Manifesting Your Heart's Desire
Book I

Fred Fengler
Todd Varnum

Heartlight Publishing

An earlier version of this book was published in 1994 with the title *Manifesting Your Heart's Desire.* ISBN 0-9641305-0-5
Second printing in 1997
This book has been revised and updated.

Published by HeartLight Publishing

ISBN 0-9641305-2-1

Cover Design by Steve Redmond
Book Design by Mark Wanner
Edited by Carol Rutter

Contents

Preface to the Second Edition

We wrote the first edition of *Manifesting Your Heart's Desire* drawing for the most part on the collective experiences of a core group who took part in the first year of the manifestation project. Many participants continued on for another two years and were joined by others, who contributed fresh and varied concepts and stories.

Our material expanded with the addition of an email discussion group, originating from correspondence generated through our website. Our readers wanted to not only correspond with us, but also have a forum to share experiences with others of like mind. After the second year, the group essentially relocated from our home to the Internet, attracting people from all over the United States and from as far away as Australia.

Another valuable information source came from a University of Vermont sociology course. One project involved students who kept journals of their techniques and outcomes. Class discussions and student essays gave us new examples to draw on.

Together and separately, we also hosted individual talks and ongoing workshops, which harvested further enlightening perspectives.

When it came time for a third printing, not only did we have a lot of new examples to utilize, but our own comprehension and interpretative powers had also evolved. Without disturbing the essential intent and flow of the original text, we incorporated some of this new material.

As we go to press today, many original participants have scattered. But others—through Internet discussion groups, workshops, and the college classroom—inspire us to continually upgrade our own insights into this fascinating phenomenon.

We are frequently reminded of the enormous implications of everyone knowing—individually and collectively—that we have the power to create what we want for ourselves, for others, for our society, and for the planet as a whole.

Fred Fengler and Todd Varnum
Burlington, Vermont
October 2001

Manifesting Your Heart's Desire
Book I

Chapter 1

An Invitation

Can we really get what we want? Can we influence outcomes? Is it possible to think about something intently and listen to our intuition to have it manifest in a timely fashion? The answer is yes! The following stories illustrate the power of mind over matter and get to the heart of this issue.

Mind Over Matter

Frank's Roofer and Contractor

Although Frank used his garage only to store wood and gardening tools, the leaking roof annoyed him. It was spring and Frank decided to install new shingles that summer. He didn't care when the work was done as long as it wasn't too expensive. He often imagined how the new roof would look, but he took no further action except to chat with a neighbor about the needed shingles.

About a month after he decided to have the roof repaired, someone knocked on his door. A roofer who had been working in the neighborhood heard that Frank wanted some work done. The roofer said he would be willing to do it for around $1,000 and could start in two weeks. Frank recalls:

> I remember thanking him and taking his business card, but I felt cautious about making a

commitment. Something did not feel right. $1,000 was a lot of money. Anyhow, I saw no need to rush. It was still early in the summer. I felt quite relaxed and confident about the job being finished over the summer.

A week later a laid-off local carpenter dropped by. He was going from house to house seeking fix-it jobs. Frank showed him the garage roof. He estimated $500, including materials, and could begin the next day. Frank told him to go ahead.

He completed the job within three days and Frank thought that the quality of workmanship was excellent.

No roofers or carpenters ever came to Frank's door in the 15 years he lived there. Nor did any come in the three years following the repair—with one exception. That same summer Frank's back porch needed a new set of wooden steps. The old ones were rotting and potentially danger-ous. Within a few weeks, a different laid-off carpenter asked for work and the process was repeated.

Tom's Consultant

Tom needed to find a consultant. His friends recom-mended a man whose qualifications seemed perfect, except that he was living somewhere in California, 3,000 miles away. Tom had heard he occasionally came to town and stayed with a friend. It became increasingly clear that he should meet this consultant. Tom remembers:

> It didn't take a moment to formulate this clear intention. It was not that I wanted to meet him but that I was going to meet him; I had a strong intuitive knowing. I had no concept of how this would happen . . . I had created a space and knew it would happen I had this desire and al-lowed it to happen. I trusted and let go.

Four days later, a woman approached Tom at a class he attended. She began telling him about an interesting man she met the night before who had just come to town from California. She added, "I don't know why I am telling you this." Tom realized she might be talking about the consultant.

"Is his name Tony Kesnovich?" he asked.

She looked surprised. "Yes. How did you know?"

Tom replied, "Oh, I've heard about Tony. I've been wanting to connect with him."

She gave him the consultant's local phone number and Tom arranged a meeting for the following Friday. Later Tom found out that Tony had been in town for only a few days.

The whole process, from voicing the desire to their first meeting, took one week.

Dot's Russian Doll

Dot always loved a certain kind of Russian doll that represented the theme of the *Wizard of Oz*. She planned to buy one locally, but the store changed hands and no longer carried it. She had no idea how to find it. "I always had it in the back of my mind to get one for myself and one for my niece, who also collects dolls."

Two years later, she was window-shopping in a neighboring state. A companion grabbed her sleeve and pointed to the doll. The shopkeeper told her she received only two of these dolls, and that they arrived at the store just two days earlier. The shopkeeper purchased them on a whim. With much joy, Dot bought both dolls.

Sarah's Cabaret Show

When Sarah learned that the evening's cabaret performance was sold out, she was upset because she had looked forward to it so much. She was told that she should not count on a cancellation because of the long waiting list.

When she got home that evening, a message on her answering machine told her about a cancellation. Since they couldn't reach her, the ticket went to someone else.

Somehow Sarah knew she was meant to see that show. Although disappointed she had missed the phone call, she met a friend at the door to find out about "no shows." At first the hostess said "no," but Sarah asked her to check again. The hostess walked around the room looking at the seating capacity for all the tables. When she returned, she told them she found two unfilled seats at the head table, directly in front of the performance. Sarah described them as the "best seats in the house!"

Reflecting on her state of mind on the day of the performance, Sarah said she just knew she would see the show. Sarah adds:

> I believe that consistent desire, unfailing trust regardless of external appearances, and perseverance are key factors in manifesting goals. I just didn't give up; I kept the desire alive. But I was not burdened with the obsession that it had to happen. I just knew that if it were right it would happen.

Coincidence or Creation?

Did these four people actually create the circumstances that resulted in the realization of their desires? Was it just coincidence that Frank was home to answer the door when the roof repairman happened to come by? How did he "know" to wait for the second repairman? Why was the roof repairman looking for work just when his services were needed? And how did he select which blocks or homes in a city of 40,000 to approach for jobs?

One might argue that over the course of two years Dot would find a store selling such a specialized doll. Yet Dot could not believe her good fortune to discover that store two days after the dolls had arrived. Had she visited three days earlier, they would not have been there. Had she come later, someone else might have bought them. She also happened to have a friend who noticed them. And how coincidental that the shopkeeper ordered two of these unusual dolls and both were still available.

Tom also believed that he would connect with the consultant, without knowing consciously how. Sarah had no doubt that she would see the concert, even though external events should have discouraged her. Instead, she trusted some internal state of consciousness.

Each person had no doubt that they created the experience or object of their desire, although none could explain how they did it. Tom could not have known that he would meet a stranger who would share the information he needed to locate the consultant. What motivated her to talk to him, especially about an incident that had nothing to do with the class? Frank had no idea ahead of time how his roof would be fixed. Dot might have found the dolls advertised in a mail order catalogue. Sarah might have made her reservation by phone. All were open to a variety of means to achieve their goals. They kept the end in mind and did not worry about how their objective would be realized. At some point a "leap of faith" occurred for each of them.

In his book *Synchronicity: The Bridge Between Matter and Mind*, David Peat refers to "synchronicity" as events that defy "our appeal to a 'scientific' view of nature." The essence of synchronicity is one's certainty that so-called coincidental events are personally meaningful. An outsider could probably explain all these incidents in terms of scientific probability or causality. But the person who experiences them rarely doubts the connection. Whether one actually creates the coincidence or participates in an apparently divine pattern depends on that individual's belief system. Each of these four people is certain that the events were meaningfully linked.

Do Our Beliefs Create Experiences?

Tim's Inclement Vacations

Every summer Tim went sailing for two weeks. It seemed that every year the weather was miserable, no matter what two weeks he chose. One summer he invited a friend to share the second week of his vacation. Just as he expected, it rained off and on most of that first week. To make matters worse, mild breezes made sailing unlikely.

When his friend arrived on board, the weather cleared and the wind picked up. Tim was absolutely amazed. The first words to his friend were, "Boy, are you lucky!" His friend turned to him calmly. "I always have good weather on my vacation," he said, as if it were no big deal.

How could this be? Was Tim always unlucky and were his friend always lucky? Could his friend control the elements? Tim remembers how his parents always seemed to experience bad weather also. He still remembers his father saying, "Wouldn't you know that these are the two days of vacation I have all year and it rains." Even when his family did experience some good weather, he remembers his father complaining about the nasty days.

Tim suddenly realized his friend's ability to always have good weather was not extraordinary. Both he and his friend were equally powerful in obtaining what they expected. They just created different kinds of conditions. Tim expected bad weather and was "rewarded" with rain and heat, just as his friend who always got good weather experienced sunshine and pleasant temperatures. In that moment, Tim understood that this was not a given but a choice.

This realization allowed Tim to change his beliefs. From that moment on, he also enjoyed constant sunshine on vacation. Not having this insight, his parents continued to tolerate unpleasant weather on their holidays. Tim notes that he and his parents were equally powerful in realizing their expectations. The outward manifestation of weather conditions clearly conformed to their beliefs. When the expectation changed, as it did for Tim, outward conditions also changed.

Jessica's "Bad Weather" Brother

Another example came from Jessica who was inspired enough by Tim's story to write to us. In her case, her brother John seemed to bring bad weather to family gatherings. So Jessica was determined to change a long-held family expectation about her "bad weather" brother. Jessica wrote:

I got a kick out of the story about the man who always manifested bad weather on vacation. That sounds exactly like my brother John. I can't remember a time when he didn't have rain on vacation.

The craziest part is that our family can be on vacation with perfect weather and when John arrives he always seems to bring clouds with him. Our entire family yells at him, but he accepts it now. I recently received a phone call from John that he is planning to see me this weekend. I was so excited when I hung up, but I looked out the window and it was pouring rain. I wanted him to come, but didn't want it to rain all weekend.

I decided to manifest perfect weather. I visualized the sun shining so brightly that I had to squint. Every time I thought about John coming, I pictured this scene in my head. Well sure

enough John arrived and the rain slowly
stopped. The next morning we woke up to the
prettiest fall day. I was so amazed because the
weather is rarely pleasant when John visits. I
told him to thank me for the beautiful weather.
He gave me a strange look and laughed at me.

It is interesting that, in the example, there is a collective belief that the arrival of a family member brings bad weather. In a sense, this suggests that when this family gathers together, they may be reinforcing the "bad weather" expectation of the brother.

Visualization in Athletics

Paul's Tennis Game

As Paul turned fifty, he realized he had to change his tennis game. No longer did he seem to have the power of his younger days. Worse still, he had developed an annoying discomfort called "tennis elbow." Sometimes he could not pick up an object without feeling pain in his right arm for days after playing. He did not want to be dependent on cortisone shots, so he considered giving up the game. He developed new tactics to reduce the tendon flare up in his elbow.

About the time these thoughts took shape, his sons gave him two books they felt would help. The first was *The Inner Game of Tennis* by W. Timothy Gallwey. The second was *Tennis: The Mind Game*. Both books stressed the power of values and belief systems and how they affect performance. His emotional state and ability to move beyond thought, analysis, and self-judgment were crucial components for improvement. Visualization techniques that he mentally rehearsed during peak performance periods prepared him for actual play.

Paul also read about experiments using the mind as a critical component in enhancing athletic skills. One study involved basketball players who wanted to improve their foul-shooting ability. Three groups of equally able players took part in the experiment. The first group shot free throws for 20 minutes a day for six weeks. The second group visualized themselves shooting perfectly for the same amount of time. The third group neither visualized nor practiced. After six weeks, the group that practiced improved 24 percent. The visualizing group improved 23 percent. The non-practicing, non-visualizing group did not improve. In other words, the players who visually rehearsed—or practiced only in their minds—did almost as well as those who practiced.

Similar experiments have been done with dart players and researchers studying world-class Soviet athletes found that combining practice and visualization was particularly successful. This was especially true when the mix favored mental exercises over actual practices (say 75 percent to 25 percent). The major reason "such relaxed visualizations have such a powerful influence on our lives," suggest the basketball researchers, "is that the body doesn't know the difference between what is real and what is imagined."

Reading these accounts helped Paul to change his own belief about the inevitability of his condition. If the body believed it had practiced a particular skill, perhaps it could also be taught to heal itself.

Mind Power in Medicine

Carl's Twisted Ankle

Carl, a university professor, felt a sharp stab of pain as he stepped off the speaker's dais. His twisted left ankle became swollen and painful as the afternoon progressed.

He barely hobbled home that evening and sank into his easy chair, preparing for more pain and stiffness the following day.

> I thought of ice and heating pads but then decided I would use my newly acquired visualization tools to bring down the swelling. Every half-hour or so, I visualized myself climbing the stairs to bed in comfort. I also saw the swelling decrease. By the time I went to bed, I had only minimal discomfort.
>
> The next morning only a hint of any discomfort reminded me of the injury. Perhaps a complete cure would have overtaxed my belief in self-healing. Of course, it might have healed anyway. I had twisted ankles before but none had ever healed this rapidly. Perhaps I did not damage it as much this time as I thought. Maybe if I had twisted my other ankle I could have used it as a control. And so goes the mind of a scientist.

Of course Carl's personal experiment did not have the control and sample size that other researchers use to study the healing properties of mind over body.

Placebos have long been noted for their effectiveness in curing disease or disability. In one study, hospitalized patients with bleeding ulcers improved markedly compared with a control group when the doctor assured them that an injection of distilled water was a new medicine that would cure them.

In another study, patients at San Francisco General Hospital were assigned to either a home prayer alliance or to a group not remembering them in prayer. It was a random double-blind study in which neither patients nor doctors knew which group a given patient was in. The prayer groups were given names and asked to pray each day for an unknown specific patient. The results? The prayed-for patients were one-fifth as likely to require antibiotics, and less likely to develop complications or die. In his evaluation, Larry Dossey M.D. in *Recovering theSoul*, comments, "If the technique being studied had been a new drug or surgical procedure instead of prayer, it would have been heralded as some sort of breakthrough."

In his popular book *Quantum Healing,* Deepak Chopra, a practicing endocrinologist, reports on several studies as well as many of his own cases of cancer patients who had "spontaneous remissions." He reports that patient attitudes about their illnesses changed prior to remission. They found some way to maintain optimism and courage, often despite their physicians' pronouncement of hopelessness. In contrast, people in a "climate of negativity" have greatly reduced abilities to heal. "Research on spontaneous cancer cures conducted in both the United States and Japan has shown that just before the cure appears, almost every patient experiences a dramatic shift in awareness. He knows that he will be healed, and he feels that the force responsible is inside himself but not limited to him." Chopra concludes, "Your body is the physical picture in 3-D of what you are thinking."

Developing Awareness of Your Power to Create

When Tom experienced bad weather, he could have called it bad luck or fate, or perhaps even blamed the weatherman. But Tom decided to change this pattern through a transformation in the way he perceived himself and his experience. Carl decided to focus on "seeing" his swollen ankle heal quickly. Both created a new result—a new experience that matched their desires. Attention to altering thoughts and beliefs changed the outward manifestation.

To manifest is to transform thoughts, beliefs, ideas, and even fantasies into objective reality where our senses can experience them. Sometimes we do this consciously. More often it's unconscious, and it may take some effort to discover the thought pattern preceding the manifested experience or object. This is a simple concept to understand but it is not always easy to put into practice. Old habits of belief and perception die hard.

Assuming responsibility for what manifests can be challenging, particularly if for a lifetime we have been socialized to look outside for satisfaction. Yet, through an awareness of what our beliefs are and how they operate and manifest we can enjoy real freedom. Then we no longer rely on some outside power, like a person or circumstance. We can independently satisfy needs and create happiness.

In this book, we journey down a path of discovery, exploring these concepts and how they operate in everyday life. We learn how to create parking places just where we want them, how to manifest the perfect job, and how to attract the mate we've always wanted.

A Manifestation Group

Twenty people accompany us on this journey. For one year, they put aside their belief that much of what happens is outside their control. For this period they "tried on" the belief in self-responsibility.

The participants represent a variety of occupational backgrounds: sales persons, secretaries, an artist, dance teacher, computer repairman, retired chemist, nurse, teacher, editor, house cleaner, engineer, and interior designer. Almost all have at least some college education.

About half belong to and attend a church or synagogue. About a third are married, half are divorced, or separated and the remainder never married. The median age is 45, but overall, the ages range from 25 to 65. Though most participants rated their health "good" or "excellent," only half used these terms to describe their financial situations. Also, three-quarters of the group were female. Perhaps this imbalance supports the stereotype of males as feeling more comfortable with processes involving the senses and external activity rather than more intuitive approaches.

The participants had many different reasons for attending. Some were simply attracted to self-growth principles. They saw the group as an opportunity to develop spiritual expansion and awareness. Another person saw this occasion as an extension of a lifelong process of growth. Janice describes it this way:

> On some level, I have been on a spiritual search since I was a little girl. In the past few years I have suddenly met people with whom I could share the feelings and questions I've had inside for so long and who have had valuable information and insights to share.

> I feel like I was drawn to this project as the next step in heightened awareness. It's so wonderful to be in such a safe and accepting group. I feel like my mind and soul are expanding.

Most participants were more specific: They wanted to learn about a process that they had always suspected operated in their lives, or were looking for a way to advance their previously sporadic manifestation practices. "I feel I need to put more time and conscious effort into it," said one. "I need the support of a group and the discipline of writing." Another person believed, "that we do manifest our lives negatively or positively via our thoughts, and I imagined it would be fun to prove it."

One group member had been using this process but hoped "the discipline involved here helps me to accomplish my goals." The project addressed a desire to find support and like-minded people for a process that one participant already "knew" was operating in her life. She reports:

> I feel like I have been constantly pulled in this direction since childhood and now it is all coming home to roost. I have been occasionally struck by my powers of wishing and willing and often shied away from believing in them because of the culture. About eight to ten years ago, when I began to meditate, my life really changed because of what I manifested. Getting into this project was also a manifestation.

All members entered the group with some belief in the effectiveness of manifestation, but within this general framework was a wide range of doubt and qualification. Some had successfully manifested for years. "I always believe that if you want something hard enough and power it up enough you can have it." Another person believes that attitude "has everything to do with how she experiences the world. I believe a person creates her own reality." Some mention the importance of visualizing what they want and having faith. As one points out, "Your whole being must not have any fear."

Others mention examples when they "knew" they had created their experience and now wanted to become more conscious of this process and expand its usefulness. An artist notes that when he took the time to write and visualize, "Art jobs suddenly popped out of nowhere." He hopes to encourage himself "to ask more questions and keep a journal." And still another said he visualized his girlfriend about two months before he met her. "She was exactly to a tee what I described."

An amusing incident happened to a woman who kept visualizing renovations that she could not afford. After about a year of "off-and-on" visualizations, a broken water hose flooded the areas needing renovation. Her insurance company covered the costs for the entire repair work, including the changes she wanted. She never visualized how the renovation would be done or financed. She simply imagined how the home would appear after the work was done.

Another participant wanted to work for a small publisher. Through several synchronous events of being in the right place at an opportune time, he got the job. In another experience he reported how he also blamed his boss or wife for making his life difficult. "When they left my life I found I was still creating much unhappiness **so I knew I was the creator of those emotions.**" This is an interesting illustration of how we learn responsibility for negative as well as positive events.

Many participants expressed doubts about their own abilities as well as about the process itself. "My intellect understands manifesting," said one, "but the rest of my being is still in the process of accepting this." Another person wanted to believe it "because it makes the most sense of any model I've seen," but she needed to demonstrate its effectiveness. Still another thought "some things are out of our control. But I would like to be convinced that everything is under our control."

Others felt one could manifest certain objects or experiences but they were uncertain how far this could be taken.

> It has been easier to manifest new gloves, trips
> abroad, and a new apartment than to create a

relationship. That seems much more elusive.

> To some degree I believe we make things happen, yet some happenings are out of our control. I'm still not sure I can make a lost cassette tape reappear. I need more proof.

A participant who doubted her own abilities and "worthiness" to have what she desired looked for support, encouragement, and guidance from the group.

> On some level I always knew that it was up to me to create what I wanted. I always felt too fearful and unworthy to try it. However, now I'm determined to take responsibility for improving my life. I believe this project will provide a good avenue to pursue my goals.

As we see in later sections, faith in one's own abilities and a feeling of deservedness are essential conditions for successful manifestions.

Finally, some group members—who had been only vaguely conscious about manifestation—wanted to explore this more objectively. Several participants were occasionally aware of synchronistic patterns. As one person noted: "I haven't done any conscious manifesting. However at times, something I thought about came into being in a way that suggested I was at the right place at the right time." Noted another subject, "What I believe usually happens, good or bad. Lately, I manifested goals I haven't given a lot of thought to. I might describe something I want, forget about it, and later it would materialize." The process of "forgetting" or detaching is another condition we explore later.

At the beginning, the participants shared certain qualities. First, **open-mindedness** along with faith and trust was essential. Second, a **willingness** to be flexible, to experiment, and try new ways of looking at life. Life itself became the laboratory and each person became both participant and observer. Finally, **commitment** to one's own expanding consciousness, the sharing of information with others, and embracing the discipline of regular record keeping were also necessary components.

At the outset, many people wanted structure and a supportive setting. With our guidance, they agreed to discipline themselves by following certain broad guidelines and procedures of observation and record keeping: Their first responsibility was to become aware of their own personal process. Second, they shared their experiences and learning in monthly meetings with the authors and other participants. Group members used journals or tapes to record manifestations, describe their own process, and comment on successes. We (the authors) were doing our own similar process, so we considered ourselves both students and teachers. During the monthly meetings, participants shared experiences and information that could lead to new perceptions and styles of manifesting. As the group coordinators, we encouraged participants to surpass self-imposed beliefs. We discussed what was and was not possible but also respected everyone's own pace and comfort level. "Playing" with the process was a theme and we even did some group experimenting around parking places, experiences that we discuss in the next chapter. One could either spend considerable time and energy or very little. Why not try both and see what happens? A person with substantial doubts about his ability to create a "perfect" job or ideal mate could start with smaller goals and later advance to larger ones. With practice, one can replace disbelief and doubt with new beliefs about success and worthiness.

The proof was in the outcomes and experiences. The only thing we stressed as coordinators was that the participants faithfully record experiences and what they observed, felt, and learned. We all agreed on one assumption, at least temporarily: We have the power to create many events in our lives.

Our Beliefs Direct Our Experience

Many participants were not even aware what their beliefs were or how they were reflected in their lives. Sometimes they had to look at events and then work back to discover the beliefs that created those events. Occasionally they found conflicting personal beliefs. For example, Paul knew about the mind's power to heal because he read of the experiments reviewed earlier. Yet, on another level, he felt only a doctor and a prescribed medication could cure his illness or disability.

All belief systems create limits. Until 1954, nearly everyone thought running a four-minute mile was impossible. Yet once Roger Bannister broke that barrier, many runners were able to repeat his achievement. We can exchange one belief system for another with fewer limits. By becoming aware of our own thoughts and the way they create our experiences, we can increase self-empowerment and control.

In a recent publication on overcoming addictions, the *Serenity Principle*, Joseph Bailey urges us to become conscious that we are not our own thoughts but the creators of our thoughts. Our belief system is not the "self," he writes, but "a filter through which we interpret life." We tend to look for and find whatever validated our previous view of reality. "When we are unaware that our thoughts create reality," says Bailey, "we become victims of our belief system and can only respond through our habits." It is not our problems or our past experiences in themselves that cause unhappiness. The cause is how we choose to perceive an event or experience. When we realize that our thoughts, beliefs and perceptions are voluntary we are free to create positive thoughts and thus positive experiences.

Only Experience Will Truly Convince

When Sally thinks back to the first time she really felt she created a desired objective through thought, she was only just beginning see its power. These events took several months to unfold but she had no doubt she created it all, even if she could not understand the process or scientifically validate it.

> I taped *Amadeus* that has a particular scene extracted from the opera *The Abduction from the Seraglio*. Only a small portion of an aria was presented in the film. Night after night I played it back while still hoping to hear not only the whole aria but also the entire opera some day. I was not obsessed; it was just a gentle desire. My enthusiasm waned somewhat over time as other events and musical experiences captured my fancy but I still remembered this experience.

On a Sunday morning—about six months after first seeing *Amadeus*—Sally tuned in to a classical music broadcast just when they introduced a new selection. She almost never listened to this station on Sunday morning.

> At the moment I tuned in, they announced upcoming highlights from *Abduction from the Seraglio*. Had I tuned in a few minutes later I might never have known what I was listening to and certainly would not have recorded it, since I only knew the one short aria. Also, I had an errand

to do during the broadcast, and would probably
have turned off the radio before going out. As it
turned out, I recorded it while I was away. Three
months later the entire production was telecast
on two public TV stations. Again, I just "happened" to notice the newspaper's TV section. I
do not regularly consult TV listings. Furthermore, three months later a classmate told me
that a live production of this opera was being
performed in Montreal about a two-hour drive
from home. I should mention that this is not one
of Mozart's most popular operas.

To an outsider, all these experiences could be happen-
stance. However, Sally had no doubt that these were not
coincidences. The wonder of the unfoldment and the associated feelings of awe and joy were impossible to convey in
words, she told us. She simply "knew" that her desire and
the manifestation were connected. Once she recognized it,
she began to see this pattern again and again.

For this reason, we encourage you to experiment with
the process yourself. This book does not persuade with
masses of verifiable evidence, as a scientific report might
try to do. Yet if you are open to experimentation, willing to
explore your own beliefs, and committed to be creator rather
than victim, then you will convince yourself of your own
power. You are the best observer, experimenter, and scientist. As you read about the participants' experiences, you
should learn that many methods account for successful
manifestations. We invite you to join us on a journey, one
that can result in a newfound awareness of your own power
and creativity. You have an opportunity to share the tri-
umphs and setbacks, insights and techniques and, most of
all, the transformations of self and perception that this

group experienced over the course of a year. However, it won't be the stories or incidents that convince you of the power of thought. Only your willingness to take responsibility for your thoughts and try actual exercises will ultimately prove the value of the process. So enjoy the accounts of others and use them as inspiration for your own exercises. Use whatever information seems most helpful, while not being limited by what is presented, in your own personal quest for self-empowerment.

Chapter 2

Manifesting For Fun

So how do we begin manifesting what we want? In this chapter we start out in a playful, lighthearted manner. We begin by observing how thoughts and experiences are linked together. For example, perhaps you were thinking of someone one morning—whom you hadn't seen in a long time—and just happened to run into her that afternoon. You might also try out a few manifestations whose outcome isn't too important, such as parking on a very busy street. These are enjoyable introductory exercises.

Then, in the next chapter, we explore manifesting in greater detail, revisiting some concepts, such as visualization, that we introduce in this chapter. After playing with simple and easy manifestations, we then learn what we can do with something intricate or charged with significance. We need to recognize and understand the most useful principles for manifesting something as substantial and complex as a relationship or a job, and why a successful outcome is so important.

Small and Inconsequential Manifestations

First, let's get our feet wet and play with manifesting in everyday life. Remember that you need not follow hard-and-fast techniques or cardinal rules. Just be open to the possibility that you can materialize your desires. As mentioned earlier, pretending that you have this power can be sufficient to get started. Play with this principle and watch for results. Experiment and observe outcomes. Keeping a daily journal of experiences and observations encourages a routine of daily practices and provides a record of successes.

Manifesting should be fun, so don't try too hard. Even when things don't seem to work out, pay attention to the peripheral conditions. When manifesting, were you happy, sad, anxious, or desperate? What mood do you seem to be in when you are most successful? Become a self-observer, but do it with a sense of curiosity and fun.

At the beginning, your goal should be clear. Target something that gives immediate feedback, one with little emotion invested in a particular outcome. That is, whether you get what you desire or not doesn't affect how you feel about yourself or your life. Also, pick something that is unlikely to happen just by chance but is still well within your belief system of possible outcomes. If you select a goal that you perceive as absolutely impossible to achieve through your own will power, then this belief sabotages the manifestation.

Our group found that the easiest kinds of initial experiments were part of their daily routine. Life was our laboratory where we would engage power in small ways. Through such discoveries we gained confidence to move on to more challenging dreams.

Most participants began by visualizing. Probably you do this all the time without being very conscious of it. For example, most of us have an image of what we want when we go shopping. I usually visualize items while making out my grocery list. If the store is familiar, I may even picture an item in a certain area. For an article of clothing, I may visualize the color, style, and fabric as well as its likely location.

Visualizing Parking Places

For our group members, visualization was only a somewhat more conscious and focused application of this very common ability to mentally picture the desired object or experience.

Parking spots were our first experiment. Many people need a daily parking space, so we gathered plenty of evidence in a short time and few drivers have a great deal of emotion or ego attached to the outcome. (If they have—as we see later—it can affect the outcome.)

Manifestors usually chose a location where success in the past had been spotty at best; this gave them a basis for comparison. Getting these parking spaces was possible, but not probable and was a good example of something that would not likely occur by chance. Some describe their results:

> I hadn't really worked on parking before, so last Wednesday on my way here I thought I'd try it. I always ended up parking on the next block. So I pictured a space directly across from here, and concentrated on this in a very positive way. I simply decided the spot would be there. Well, I turned onto the street and the empty parking spot wasn't up or down a little but directly across from the front door!

> Every time I go to Burlington I have a tough time finding parking. I like to park at City Market. I decided on a place right in front, which of course is next to impossible. I didn't work on it too hard; I just decided it would be there. I turned the corner and there it was right in front.

I wanted to manifest the best possible spot near a location I knew would be busy on Friday night. The chances of getting it were near nil at that time. I projected a place right in front or very near by. As I drove down College Street someone backed out right across the street as I approached. Talk about energy; that was incredible!

I was manifesting the perfect place at the shopping mall entrance. I was there to participate in a Christmas concert and needed to be close. The car nearest to the entrance pulled out just when I needed it. I said, "Yes, yes!" Other drivers wanted it, but I was there first. I couldn't believe it.

I needed to get to a haircut appointment at 9, when it is almost impossible to find a space. I was running 10 minutes late, so I "put it out" and knew it would be there. I "saw" the spot right out front. It was a brief visualization. I didn't have time to run around searching. I got the only place on that block, right where I had visualized it. I loved it!

Two days after Thanksgiving, I had to go shopping and decided what spot I wanted. I pictured the fourth place down from the handicapped spot. Sure enough, I got that exact space.

Several themes characterize these successes. First, their intents were very clear. They wanted specific and convenient parking. In the last case, only one location would do.

Second, all knew from past experience that getting these spots was unlikely, but possible, just the same. All were positive they would get them and any misgivings were absent. (Later, we examine the consequences of manifesting with even a little doubt.)

Third, little effort was involved in these visualizations. One "didn't work on it too hard." For another, "it was only a brief visualization." They had confidence they would be successful. They just "knew" or "decided" the spots would be there.

Finally, almost all of them appreciated the achievement. Though confident, they still "couldn't believe it," found it "incredible," and "loved it." Doubts came back only after the experiment's conclusion. They had "parked" their doubts off to the side during this experiment.

In a variation on finding parking places, two people—who were illegally parked—visualized having no parking tickets.

> I forgot to put money in a frequently patrolled meter. I tried to visualize "no ticket" on the windshield. The parking meter froze so the arm couldn't come up. I spent a couple of additional hours downtown without a ticket. I enjoyed the freebie.

> I visualized a particular parking spot and found it. I was gone much longer than the meter allowed. I visualized a ticket-free windshield. Not only was I successful, but I also had time left on the meter.

> I parked there for almost two hours and the meter only registered about 45 minutes. A few weeks later, I manifested the same place and again I stayed longer than the money allowed.

Although the meter had expired when I returned, I didn't have a ticket.

Fun with Everyday Experiences

Opportunities constantly arise to create more joy and less effort while going about the business of daily living. Manifesting also makes life more interesting. Each situation becomes an experiment in personal power, as we see in the examples that follow. The first involves a man who enjoyed using his mind to move traffic out of his way. Using a tape recorder, he described the incidents as they happened. His enthusiasm and excitement were evident on the tape. The other incidents require little additional comment.

> The ten cars in front of me are following a large truck. I am going to expand my energy space out and have the way open up. [Pause] The truck just pulled off! I also have been losing cars and only three or four are in front of me now. One car turned into a driveway and another turned off and now no one is in front of me. It is amazing! [10 minutes later] A dump truck just pulled out in front of me. Bingo! Three miles down the road the truck turned off. It worked again. I'm all clear. [5 minutes later] Now a bucket loader is ahead. Here goes number three. This one took only thirty seconds.

> I needed to call my husband at work. In the past I usually get either a busy signal or no answer and it has really frustrated me. Today I kept getting busy signals, so I visualized the receptionist hanging up from one call to answer mine. It worked! Of all the times I've tried to call my husband in the past, I'd only reached him once.

United Parcel Service can be a zoo right before Christmas. As I was driving there I began thinking how wonderful it would be if I zipped right through. I actually visualized two people ahead of me, which at this time of year is absurd. Well much to my delight, when I walked in only two people were ahead of me. They were both being waited on, so I was the next person in line. Hurrah! I couldn't believe it but it was delightful and I was very grateful.

Lately I have this annoying bladder problem: In the middle of a movie at a theater, I have to run out to go to the bathroom, especially if I've had a drink first. A couple of weeks ago I had dinner at a Chinese restaurant including a beer and some tea. Just as the movie started I told my body that all the cells would retain water and my bladder would remain empty. I felt confident that my body could do this.

Well, I didn't even have to go to the bathroom after. My friend and I went to a bar for a drink. I still didn't have to go. I got home hours later and still didn't have to go! I tried this last week and it worked again. This will become an opening-credit movie ritual from now on.

A footnote to the incident with UPS: This experimenter also tried visualization at UPS on a second occasion. This time she visualized only one person ahead of her. (Perhaps her previous experience gave her confidence to push her belief system a bit further.) She did find just one person ahead of her, but that customer had dozens of packages. She reports, "A few moments went by. Then a second cashier appeared and I was rushed through rather quickly." She got what she had asked for, but what she really wanted was to get through quickly. She was fortunate that some part of her knew this was her real desire. Perhaps a lesson here is to be careful what you ask for; you are likely to get it.

As she left UPS, she noticed six to eight people behind her. Also, the reason she had to make a second trip so soon was suddenly clear. "The gift arrived later than expected, forcing me to go back to check on it. The second trip allowed me to experience success in getting through as I wanted to."

You can probably sense this woman's delight as she played with her power. Making a second trip—which might have been an aggravation—instead became an opportunity to repeat her previous experiment. She was challenging but not overextending her belief about what might be possible, creating only one person in line the second time instead of two. She had no overwhelming need to create a short line. Rather her attitude was, "Wouldn't it be wonderful if?"

Manifesting Objects and Articles

How often have you desired some object and not known where to find it? Then, when you're not looking, it presents itself, often in an unexpected place. Whether the item is small or large, the process is the same.

> I wanted a straw hat. I visualized it but did not give it a great deal of effort or put in a lot of detail. I knew I would run into it, perhaps at a garage sale. As I was backing out of a parking lot, I noticed a straw hat sitting in the middle of the road. I looked around but nobody was claiming it. So now I have a new straw hat and it didn't cost me anything.

I planned to have a big salad for dinner but after I got home from the store I realized I forgot to get a tomato. So I decided to manifest one. I pictured myself going into the refrigerator and seeing a tomato. I didn't give it much thought after that.

Later, I looked in the refrigerator but saw no tomato. Then a few minutes later my roommate Kate walked in with five ripe tomatoes. She had been babysitting and the family gave her tomatoes from their garden. She offered me one as soon as she arrived.

I wanted a watch pin to wear on my blouse. I can't wear a regular watch because it irritates my skin. I had never seen one for less than $25. I had put it in the 'want file' in the back of my head. I thought about it three or four times a week. It was not so much visual. I did not restrict it to how it would look. Yesterday while running into a department store to use the ladies' room, I saw it for $9.95 and had a variety to choose from.

I was invited to a formal dance and knew exactly what dress I wanted. It would be tight fitting in the upper part, then flare out, and cost less than $100. I pictured this dress but did not think about it too much. I just decided I was going to get it. I made up my mind.

I went into a store and the first one I saw was this dress in two versions—one had short sleeves and the other long. That was the only decision I had to make. The clerk said, "Get the long-sleeved one." And it was only $60. I loved it and got tons of compliments. It looked great!

———

My mom wanted a pale yellow sweater. I told her that I would be near a certain store and I bet they would have one. They had exactly what she wanted in every size but hers. At first I was bummed but then decided to ask the clerk to check out back. Sure enough she had one. The clerk acted surprised though because someone earlier had asked for the same thing, but she couldn't find one in stock then. I was surprised as well!

———

I visualized day after day the early arrival of the costumes so they would come in time for an important group picture. The company promised delivery by May 14 but I said they had to come by May 2. I put a sign on the front door of the studio on May 2 telling the deliveryman to leave the costumes at the studio. The chances of him coming on that afternoon were slim but I visualized it again and again. Of course, they arrived on May 2.

———

I wanted a sporty red car with a sunroof and stereo system, which appeals to my inner child. When I finally found the car on a Friday, the salesman was sorry but it had been promised to someone else. Over the weekend I never doubted that somehow this car was going to be mine. I envisioned it parked in my driveway. I saw myself driving it to Virginia to visit my parents.

Monday morning the dealership called. They said it was a miracle that the deal worked out. Not only had the car been promised to another customer, but the car had also been offered to a wholesale buyer who had the second option. This buyer delayed because he was reluctant to make an offer. By the time he arrived, the car was already mine.

A straw hat blowing on the street. A tomato for a salad. The perfect dress found in the first store entered. A delivery of costumes on an afternoon when delivery was unlikely. A car promised to two other people suddenly available. These individuals had no doubt they created their "luck." (Actually, no one in the group ever uses the word "luck.") The individual who wanted the red car somehow "knew it was going to be mine." And the person who expected the costume delivery was so sure it was coming on the day **she had determined it would come** that she left a sign for the deliveryman to leave it at her studio. The effort varied somewhat, from the woman who wanted the dress and "did not think about it too much" to the person who visualized the delivery "day after day."

Finally we present a manifestation involving two people. Does it hasten a manifestation if someone helps? In this case two sisters together manifested a sink. The sister who wanted it for two years affirmed a white pedestal sink in good condition at a reasonable price. "Every time I went into the bathroom I visualized the sink there." Her sister was also manifesting it at a price between $100 and $250. "I pictured myself using the sink and how it would look."

About three weeks after both sisters began in earnest, the sister who wanted the sink was driving with her husband. "My husband said, 'Think pedestal sink,' as we drove up a long hill. As we came down the other side, there it was in a yard. It was in good condition and cost $175."

For two years before joining forces and visualizing, she was unable to locate one. Doing daily visualizations, they found it within three weeks. It is also interesting that the husband intuited its location, cueing his wife in so they would not speed past it. Note also that the price was exactly halfway between the minimum and maximum amounts they envisioned.

Visualization for Athletes

In Chapter 1 we mentioned studies documenting the effectiveness of visualization for enhancing athletic abilities. This can be almost as helpful as spending the same amount of time in physical training. The body simply does not seem able to distinguish between the activity experienced and the activity vividly imagined.

> I am currently bowling as a gym requirement. I always loved bowling and practiced quite a bit in the past. However, this class is teaching me to throw differently than I'm comfortable with. After a couple of gutter balls, I decided to sit down and manifest throwing a strike with the new technique I learned from your book. After visualizing several times I tried again. I stood up; thought it through; and got a strike.

> I was so amazed that I could learn just by thinking about it. My mental practice for the short amount of time was so beneficial to my game. I was so happy to see that I could do some of the things you wrote about.

Every so often I would bring the lacrosse team together and have the girls take a few deep breaths. I would then lead them through a guided visualization of a play we were having problems with. I noticed every time we did that they were completely tuned in and things clicked. They really could do things with ease and grace. It was incredible.

This became a ritual. Before games I would lead them through a visualization of a game-related situation where they would see the ball in front of them. They picked it up perfectly, cradled it perfectly; passed it perfectly; and eventually scored. I would ask them to feel the joy of running down the field and scoring. After we did that together I would have them do it on their own quietly.

My daughter had problems riding a horse. Every night she and I both visualized riding the way the instructor told her to. This meant putting her foot in the stirrups and riding the horse holding legs and arms properly. She saw herself running with the horse and as the perfect horseback rider.

I reminded her to do it first thing when she awoke and last thing at night. We did it together for a week. Her next lesson was phenomenal. Her teacher couldn't believe how connected she was with the riding, such as how she held her hands. Remember, a week passed and she had only practiced in her mind. She was right on cue. She followed the teacher's instructions exactly. Prior to this visualization marathon, she demonstrated little progress.

One nice thing about this exercise is that you can, as with parking places, obtain direct feedback in a short time. You have a clear memory of what the problem is and recognize that practice isn't helping much. You visualize and watch for results. In the horse-riding episode, the daughter did not even have an opportunity for physical practice. Yet the teacher confirmed her progress.

Visualizing a Trip

The following student wanted to see her brother in Las Vegas but didn't have the money. She talked about it with friends and family who told her to go at Christmas break. It seemed impossible until she got an unexpected refund check. She interpreted the check as a sign that she should go. "It was at this point that I started getting serious about manifestation. I was going to Las Vegas."

The following is a fairly lengthy account but it shows a great deal of variety in the way in which visualization and other methods can be combined to enhance success. It is also worth noting how frequently she uses images as if she has already completed the manifestation. It's a "done deal."

> Sometimes I pictured myself getting off the plane and greeting my brother. It was like I planned my arrival. Most of the time these scenarios seemed so real. The visualizations took place wherever I was. I would be staring out from a car—or even on the toilet—picturing Las Vegas.
>
> Each visualization boosted my confidence. I also used daily verbal affirmations. I wrote affirmations but not that often. At times I talked to people like the trip was all planned, that I had tickets, and was prepared to take off. I sang in the shower about going and chanted it to myself

as I walked upstairs. It just became a daily routine.

Every time I phoned my brother he acted like I was coming. He would tell me what we were going to do, how many days I would stay, and where to meet him at the airport. It was like we were in a play, performing the parts of each other in Las Vegas. At times, I felt like I was already there with him. It was such a good feeling. My journal entries with simpler manifestations gave me confidence on this bigger one.

Every time a simpler one happened it made me realize the power I have over this trip.

Dreams and prayers also played a huge role. Every night I went to bed knowing that I wanted to dream about Las Vegas. I would literally plan out the dream. I dreamt of other things too, but Las Vegas always seemed to figure in. I would say a little prayer to God almost every night and they made me feel happy and more confident.

For the next few months her confidence ebbed and flowed at times. There were no more signs. Then over Thanksgiving two things happened that she hadn't planned on. First her credit card limit went up. Second, she read a brochure depicting inexpensive package deals to many destinations, including Las Vegas. As she said,

"I got butterflies in my stomach. All these weeks of manifesting the trip as well as just manifesting in my every-day life paid off. Every doubt I had about manifestation flew out the window."

What makes this story exciting—apart from its successful conclusion—is how **playful** persistence can pay dividends. She really had fun with all the creative ways to manifest. She even programmed her dreams. In fact she had fun with the entire process, a subject we return to at the end of this chapter. It is fun in and of itself to fantasize. How real are our fantasies? For her "most of the time they seemed so real."

She also mentioned how she felt she was play-acting, "like we were in a play performing the parts of each other in Las Vegas." They acted as if the trip was already a certainty. They virtually lived it in the present instead of some wishful dream in the future, which can often keep it in the future. In other words, if you manifest something to happen in the future, it always unfolds in the future.

Money and Business

How often have you thought about winning the lottery or have you just "known" enough money would be there to pay the bills? Perhaps you wonder how you can increase sales with simple visualizations. The following cases illustrate these possibilities:

> I always wanted to go to California. I clipped California pictures from magazines and "dream weaved" a story about it with me in it. I also focused on a picture of a particular hotel room I wanted to stay in. I used the room visualization as a concrete focus or symbol for the trip.

> At a wine and food festival, a grand prize of a trip to California and private vineyard tours was offered. I bought four tickets and began powering up my mental movie. About half an hour before the drawing, a little voice said to buy six more. It would not relent. Six tickets cost $24

and I only had $25 in my wallet. I bought those tickets and won the trip.

———

I've had trouble paying bills this month. The only time I really make fast cash is when I am waitressing. The past few nights I envisioned myself making a certain amount of money each night. Each time, I made the predicted amount and was able to cover the bills. That is why I don't get stressed when I think I won't have enough cash.

———

I sell advertising space. Before I approach a potential client, I imagine them happy to see me and excited about the product. I also imagine them saying "yes." It has been going so well. Before the interaction, I convey the attitude that I am going to learn about myself and meet new people. In one case I learned that we both had lived in the same city. They asked me about buying a new computer. Instead I gave them useful advice about the malfunctioning one. I get the feeling we are people who all crap in the pot. We are just human beings, so I can eliminate fear.

———

Two days ago I got a bill in the mail for one of my credit cards and it was for $274. I didn't have enough in my checking account and I wondered if I should pay just part of the bill. Then I realized that was a limitation thought. If I paid less it was like telling my subconscious to not provide me enough to pay that bill and I was willing to settle for less. I spent a moment in faith and made the check out for the full amount. In the mail the same day, I received a deposit statement for $275 which I hadn't counted on.

By the way, the individual who won the California trip also got the visualized rooms. "Both rooms were exactly as I pictured," she said, even though she and her husband arrived in California on Memorial Day Weekend without reservations.

Notice that the person who used visualizations to make a sale defused the need for success by focusing on the human qualities of potential clients. She saw them as "interesting" people who could help her learn about herself.

She had a history of negativity with some former clients, and assumed at first the new owners would express the same hostility. She caught herself doing this and instead projected a positive and friendly first meeting. Her encounter unfolded just as she envisioned it. Perhaps it would have happened without the visualization, but at the very least she gained the courage to meet the new owners instead of simply giving up.

Finally, notice how in the last incident, the person recognized that her thoughts were undermining a belief in monetary abundance. She trusted the needed funds would appear and they did, even to within one dollar of the total amount.

The Joy of Visualizing

We close this chapter with an often-overlooked satisfaction that accompanies manifestations. At times one can believe that the result is worthwhile, but the means to that end require considerable effort. Yet the endeavor itself can be very enjoyable. This next account illustrates that great pleasure arises from the process, particularly with visualization. In other words, visualization itself can be as enjoyable as the actual attainment of the goal. The journey can grant as much pleasure as the destination.

When we completely immerse ourselves in the present—experiencing the joy of the anticipated goal—two aspects facilitate its eventual emergence into physical reality. First, a great deal of positive energy infuses the physical manifestation. The emotional content behind any manifestation is also very important. As long as it does not come from a place of neediness it can only enhance the creation. Second, enjoying the process eradicates both neediness and attachment because the fantasy is satisfying in itself.

A woman was looking for a new apartment but her main desire was for specific kitchen gadgets. She had no idea at the time that she was engaged in manifestation. Note the pleasure she took in the time she spent fantasizing, often in considerable detail.

> On a scrap of paper I wrote a small list of things I really wanted. And by "want" I mean I could taste and even touch them. That's how vivid they were. My list consisted of a gorgeous wooden salad bowl with tongs, a pepper mill, and Italian specialty foods, especially packages of Italian Panettone Verdi cakes in those glossy, green boxes.

> I thought about these things so much that they consumed me. I don't know why, but I just envisioned myself making fabulous salads in my new bowl and grinding fresh pepper over it. After the fantasy meal, my guests and I would enjoy Italian cake.

> At the time, I was saving for an apartment so I didn't have enough to spend on extravagances. I still passionately thought about making sal-

ads in that bowl and cracking pepper over it. I read and reread that list on the bus and at my desk. I just sat there, almost catatonic, dreaming about it.

I had no idea I was visualizing or manifesting. I thought I was just wishfully thinking. I didn't tell anyone because I thought it would be considered miniscule.

A month later at work, a huge cake-sized box was on my chair. Someone said, "They bought us Christmas gifts." A lot of styrofoam stuffing inside covered up the gift. Guess what was in there? A beautiful tikki wood salad bowl with tongs, flavored oils and vinegar, a small pepper mill, a banana-shaped chocolate bar and a box of Verdi Panettone was in there. I looked up in amazement as I saw 150 people marveling over the same gift.

I didn't bother explaining this to anyone. I just quietly went about my day and smiled up at God because I knew that "He" knew I got it because of my faith. In my mind, I already had these things and was passionately enjoying them. In my "mind movie," I wasn't wishing or wanting; I was already enjoying them.

A Bible passage states that God gives what you believe you have already received. My best advice in manifesting is to **never worry or doubt**. Don't pray through tears and anxiety. Go to that screen in your head and play your own movie. Watch yourself enjoying the outcome that you choose. And play it over and over. Enjoy the movie freely, with all your senses. Don't tense up and worry about how you will attain it. Relax; you already have it remember?

The only things that exist are what you create from your mind. I no longer hope or wish. I believe I can have the world, and I go about my day knowing that I will receive everything that I desire.

That little salad bowl changed my life!

Conclusion

We hope by now that you have been inspired by these examples and may even have tried some manifesting of your own. Perhaps you have examples much like those you have been reading about and are looking to manifest something more challenging. Take your time before trying something complex such as a meaningful job or exciting relationship. The next chapter delves into more detail about these principles and provides a variety of concepts and techniques to choose from, particularly when pondering something more challenging.

Remember that true appreciation of your power can only come from experimentation. In this early stage, be sure to choose goals that do not contradict your belief about what is possible. Pick something just beyond what might occur by reasonable chance. Watch your desires and see what happens. Also, look at each experience or object currently in your life. Might it have originated in a previous thought? Above all, have fun in whatever you choose to manifest.

Chapter 3

Principles of Manifesting

What Goes Around Comes Around

The more you work with manifesting the more truth you see in the above subheading. Clearly, where you direct your energy is what you attract.

When we started our research in 1988, we looked at manifesting as another tool. We understood that activating this new method was a choice.

Over time, we realized that we manifest constantly. Involuntary manifestations are not really an option, but we can choose to develop awareness and learn how to use it to our advantage. We discovered that certain basic principles are central to everyone: First, "deciding what you want," then, "taking action," and finally "allowing it to happen." A great deal of individual variation occurs in implementing these steps and no single method emerges as the best. The all-purpose elixir doesn't exist because we are each on our own path.

The dynamics of manifesting don't change. Discovering your own style requires awareness of how you manifest already. With this recognition, you can choose the style that best suits you. The individual commentaries offer a myriad of approaches to mull over.

Be Clear on Your Intention

Although this sounds like the easy part, we found that many group members had trouble deciding what to manifest. Uncertainty or lack of clarity prevailed, particularly regarding larger, more complex manifestations such as relationships, jobs, or a state of being such as happiness. Many people knew more about what they didn't like or want than what they did. Sometimes it was simply a matter of affirming the opposite, such as attracting a partner who appreciated them rather than **not** having someone who always criticized them.

However, in many cases it was difficult to pinpoint the desire. This could lead to sending vague or general requests. Additionally, a mixed-message petition yields mixed results.

You always have the choice of how much detail to instill. If you know the specifics, then go ahead and manifest with those characteristics in mind. However, keep in mind that you don't absolutely need elaborate details. If unclear about the particulars, then let the Universe decide for you.

How Much Detail Is Necessary?

You now have some experience manifesting parking places and articles of clothing. You are ready to create something a bit more complex. Most previous examples have been relatively small and concrete. In fact, when starting out, most chose direct and uncomplicated goals.

> This morning I started thinking about getting a hat. Last Wednesday, I decided I was going to find a hat today—one that fits, stays on, and looks nice. Four hours later, I found it and I've never seen a hat like it before. I have about three plain straw hats, but this hat is made out of a heavier material and was reduced from $14 to $6.

———

> I wanted an affectionate toy poodle because they are not allergen causing and don't shed. I couldn't afford one from the pet shop, so I put out to the Universe that if anyone has a toy poodle they wanted to get rid of for any reason, I wanted to know about it. In less than a week I saw an ad for a female toy poodle. The owners had to find a new home for the dog because their daughter beat up on her.

These are fairly small items and do not seem to require a great deal of thought or effort. However, for some objects or experiences, you may want to be much more specific and detailed. Larger goals almost seem to invite elaboration. Taking a vacation often requires careful planning. Choosing an apartment is a big investment, both in terms of money and lifestyle.

> My Austrian ski vacation had to have great snow and sun. I want the right flight and enough money for everything. I also want good traveling weather and convenient luggage transfers. I even want fun ski companions whom I can go out with. I want to have a great time!

———

> While jogging I said, "I want a light, quiet, warm apartment." I also made a list of essentials and preferences. I pictured myself sitting high above the lake with western light on my plants, a kitchen behind me, and the bedroom located in the back. When I pictured my future apartment it felt really good!

By their own assessment, both individuals were quite successful. The apartment hunter reports, "I got all the essentials and most of the preferences. The things I hadn't listed were strange, like no square rooms and a four-foot-high closet."

This last point raises an interesting question about manifesting details. What happens to those aspects that you do not specify? Do you have "to cover all the bases," or risk receiving some features you really don't want? Here are two examples illustrating some potential problems of too much precision.

> When I wanted a clear credit card, I received an interesting offer: The company would pay off the old card if I signed up for their card at a lower rate. I switched and got exactly what I asked for—"a clear credit card." Of course, I realize now that I should have asked for a paid-off card with no debt.

> It seems that whatever lacked in one relationship would appear in the next. For example, when I was with someone who was not masculine enough, I would focus on that. Then my next encounter would be with a very masculine man. But other troublesome issues came up because I had only focused on that one quality.

> At a workshop we had to write down a goal we wanted to reach by the following year and how we would go about it. My main goal was to have a stable, fulfilling relationship. I was not desperate. Basically I had no expectations and just enjoyed the moment. Periodically I would think about what I thought might be ideal. I concluded that a relationship similar to the one I had with my best friend would be great.

Eleven days later, this man walked into the store. I realize I manifested this relationship, which is very much like the one with my best friend. What I never thought to ask for was someone who is sensuous and health conscious. This experience taught me to be more general and trust that the Universe takes care of the specifics.

I had thought that teaching cartooning as a job could be fun and profitable. It took over a year for my application to be looked at. In that period I forgot about the position and focused on my progress as a caricaturist. When the opportunity arrived, I suddenly thought of excuses for not doing it: I had no car; it would interfere with other jobs; and maybe muffle my political mouth. This is a case of attracting something you don't quite want or isn't really the best thing. Usually it takes awhile to realize it isn't for you.

I was very late going to the airport to catch a flight to Newark and then one home. I didn't think I was going to make it. On the way, I asked my friends to manifest with me that I would catch the flight to Newark. I made it because it was late departing. Unfortunately I didn't ask them to manifest that I would catch the connecting flight, so I had to spend the night in the airport.

I realized I had to visualize the final destination because I got what I wished for. Furthermore, it seemed that my subconscious didn't want me to make it all the way home that night

because some beliefs got in the way. For example
I was afraid of flying into bad thunderstorms
and I didn't want to come home to an empty
house late at night. Sometimes beliefs contradict our conscious desires.

These subjects were fairly clear on what they wanted.
Aspects of the apartment that the woman did not factor in
were "strange" but did not mar her overall satisfaction. Still,
some group members did not always know what they
wanted. In the above examples, both manifestors got just
what they "thought" they wanted, but ultimately they were
not so happy with the results. This brings up the issue of
clarity: Be careful what you select because you will attract
it to you.

The first case is just an amusing small example. The
manifestor got exactly what she asked for—to clear her
credit card. However, what she really wanted was no debt.
In the second case of the romantic partner, the subject had
not clearly established the kind of person she wanted to
attract. However, the experience furnished useful information for creating a new manifestation. Like a scientist, she
tries out several formulas until she hits upon the right one.
We can read about or tell others about the kind of relationship or job we desire. But at some point we may need to
"try on" a particular kind of relationship or job to find out if
this is a good fit.

Another woman realized she liked exotic men: "I need to
focus on a type of man I could really have a relationship
with, and not just exciting encounters." For much of her
early adult life, she liked adventurous brief flings. But when
she wanted a more stable and lasting relationship, early
desires kept interfering with her new direction. She also
had attachment and anxiety around this manifestation:
"Those small affairs seemed easy to manifest because very

little effort preceded them. A lot of emotion is deployed in searching for a soul mate."

The second person thought she wanted a relationship much like the one she had with her best friend, and she did create it. It had many admirable qualities, but she left out the strong romantic component, which was not part of the relationship with her best friend. One reaction would have been to try to be so specific that she anticipated every possibility. Her alternative reaction was to trust some higher power to take into account all her desires and needs to come up with a suitable partner.

Also, the kind of job the cartoonist wanted at one time did not appeal to him a year later. We are always evolving and sometimes experience a gap between our initial desires/projections and the eventual result. Even though he turned the job down, he probably learned something about himself and the process.

In the story about flying, the student landed in Newark, but learned a valuable lesson about asking for the ultimate desired outcome. Interestingly, she was also aware of potentially conflicting fears that may have interfered with her final destination even if she had remembered to manifest it.

As a footnote to the toy poodle story, the new pet owner later found the dog to be very destructive when left alone. The dog damaged the curtains and literally trashed the apartment one evening, necessitating that she be returned to the former owner. The manifestor had not asked for a dog that was willing to be left alone.

One recently divorced group member drew up a list of desirable characteristics in a new partner. He fantasized what it would be like to meet such a woman. Within a couple of months, he met an attractive and compatible colleague. She shared his interests, loved sports and music, and enjoyed playing tennis on a regular basis.

Had I been recording manifestations then, I would have seen that she almost perfectly matched my checklist. However, one characteristic I had left off the list was sexual orientation. Much to my frustration, she was a lesbian.

How do we deal with getting more than we bargained for? After all, it is almost impossible to cover all contingencies ahead of time.

Some manifestors omitted many specifics about the desired object or experience. Instead they focused on a central feeling of what it would be like to have the object or experience. How would you feel if you just obtained your desire? A similar approach is simply to **trust** that some higher power or authority—either within you or outside—knows what is best.

I am living more out of trusting the process than consciously trying to shape the future, which is new for me. I think I tried too hard to maintain conscious control. I now feel that my best course is to manifest in generalities because I want to be open to possibilities that may be much greater than what I could envision on my own.

Whenever I describe some specific interests I wish to share with an ideal partner, I always make sure to include some general characteristics such as shared joy, laughter, and all forms of intimacy and companionship. I still include the most important specifics, but I also try to imagine what it **feels** like to be in an ideal relationship. I try to remain open to possibilities that could give me enjoyment and stimulation.

When you decide to manifest a detailed laundry list, another consideration is whether those desired elements come from intrinsic needs or outside expectations. For example, one woman wanted a job that would not interfere with the time her husband worked or the time when her children would be home from school. She also wanted a good salary so she could supplement her husband's income. She found a job that fit these criteria exactly, yet she eventually turned it down because it involved fundraising, which would be stressful. She then found a job working within a school system that also had these characteristics, but she quit after one year. Eventually, she realized that the job had to be interesting and challenging to her, and she began to focus less exclusively on what she thought her family needed.

So often we look outside to the needs of others—or to the values expressed within our culture—for guidance in choosing appropriate goals. When we ignore internal interests and desires, we feel dissatisfied and confused.

Later, we discuss the value of what we can learn, even when the desired manifestation does not work out as expected. Attaining goals is really only a small part of the pleasure, because manifesting today's goal only leads to new desires tomorrow. As we appreciate what we learn from the process, we add a great deal of adventure and enjoyment to life.

Although he felt frustrated at first, the man—who ended up with a gay woman's friendship instead of a romance—learned platonic intimacy, which helped him relate to straight women as well. Over time, he developed wonderful close friendships with women, which helped alleviate loneliness and provide some of the companionship he originally believed could only come from romance. He also developed empathy and emotional intimacy that made him attractive to women who were looking for that in a romantic context. We can address our desires in many forms, if we do not limit ourselves.

If you are not sure exactly what characteristics you want, let the Universe do the work for you. If you are concerned about leaving out some element or not covering all the bases, you don't have to spend vast amounts of time constructing a detailed wish list. Move to a higher or more general level of manifesting. Experience the goal as already achieved and the satisfaction and happiness that you would feel at this time.

The more we focus on what we want and the less we direct the solution, the more options the Universe has to present. It's surprising how creative the Universe can get.

Power Up Your Creation

Okay, let's assume you now know what you want. You also decided to either describe in detail your desired manifestation, or simply experience a state of happiness about its outcome, trusting the Universe to fill in the blanks.

Now you must select a method to attract it. Once again, you might wish to experiment with options. Visualization, affirmations, and emotional identification are three popular techniques. "Powering up" energy with any of these methods fortifies your resolve and chances of success.

Once again, remember that you manifest all the time whether you pay attention or not. However, you have the choice to direct energy into avenues supporting what you want and to weaken energies that bring what you don't want. The following techniques help to focus and power up energy so it attracts what you desire. You may wish to use these methods alone or in combination with each other.

Visualization

In Chapter 2, we explored a wide range of experiences. Most of them used some form of visualization, the most popular technique. Participants created a picture of the desired outcomes. They visualized, for example, "being open and loving while teaching," "a sporty red car in my driveway," "happy clients," "how to cradle and pass at the same time," and "cells retaining water so my bladder would remain empty."

Each person achieved the goal, in most cases with minimal effort. One participant reported, "For smaller, less potent visualizations, sometimes all it takes is a well-thought out flicker in the mind." Another said that for a minor goal, "I just see it happening in my mind's eye and then keep my real eyes open to recognize the results. If I want to talk to someone, I 'see' that person dialing my number. Usually they do."

One woman feared announcing her resignation to her boss. She realized that, "by expecting negativity that is what I would create."

> I pictured pink light, which is the color of love, all through my boss and the situation. I pictured giving up my fears and hugging her. It was fantastic. She talked to me for over an hour about how she understood where I was now in life and admitted she didn't want me to leave.

The salesperson also employed this technique before approaching a client. She visualized them "happy to see me and excited about my project and saying 'yes' to my sale."

Another person used a powered-up visualization to get rid of unwanted guests. She called this her "broom technique."

> Three people wanted to stay the night in my house. They were from another part of the state and had business in the area the next morning. However, the timing was poor, so I visualized sweeping these people out. It turned out that the engagement they had the next day was canceled.

This is an interesting case because it required the cooperation of a third party, the person with whom they had the appointment, their main reason for staying at her house.

> One fun story of our trip to Sedona involved my sister who wanted a large crystal that cost $200. She could only afford $30, so I visualized her getting a large crystal for $30. The next day when we were in the store again she found a stone she loved. She asked the guy the price and he looked her right in the eyes and said "for you it's $30." Wow, that blew us away! We hummed the Twilight Zone melody for a while after that.

One thing that makes this visualization noteworthy is that the friend manifested the crystal. Sometimes manifesting for someone else is easier, because ego is not involved and the friend usually has less attachment. Two friends might find greater success manifesting for each other than they could on their own.

If you have some difficulty visualizing what you want, you might use pictures from magazines or photographs to remind you of your desired object and provide a concrete focus. In the last chapter we discussed a person who clipped "California pictures from a magazine" and a "picture of a particular hotel room I wanted to stay in."

Another person took a photo of a desired condo unit and taped it to his refrigerator so he would see it every day. He actually ended up in a condo unit close by and with features even more desirable than he had originally imagined. What he couldn't see at the time, was that he would marry (a different manifestation) and his list would modify as his circumstances changed. Sometimes we end up getting what we really want even if we weren't aware initially. It is an ongoing process and good to not be too rigid in our desires.

That leaves us open to receive something even better than we originally intended.

Daydreams and Fantasies

Daydreams can be a form of manifesting, though we usually view them as somewhat lighter and less directed. They can be wide-ranging and almost random in nature with little thought of implementation. Nevertheless, daydreams can have the power to create. The following example suggests that we pay attention to fleeting fantasies. The first account warns us to become more aware of daydreams. The second demonstrates how it can work even without awareness of how it evolved.

> I visualize things pretty easily and learned that it's important to monitor daydreams. Sometimes what we daydream (good or bad) sets the scene into motion. So, like the words we speak carry power and momentum so do daydreams. Therefore, when we find ourselves in a negative "what if" kind of daydream, we must quickly abort and replace it with a powerful, positive visualization. This happened a couple of times and taught me that everything in our lives truly does start with the mind.

> About four years ago I was in a frustrating marriage. I was also very career and money-oriented. I grew angry when I came home and my husband had spent the day drinking or playing golf when there was so much to do! By this time, I was six months pregnant and felt I was carrying the whole load. I remember saying to a co-worker "My husband needs some twenty-year-old bimbo, not me!" I said it a number of times

and actually daydreamed about catching him with someone in the act. I really didn't want my marriage to end, just to change. However, I put out the wrong message.

Three months later my husband said that he didn't think he loved me. My suspicion was so keen, that I knew exactly where he was without spying, plus he never told me anything. One day he said he was going out for a few hours and would be back by 3:00. When he wasn't home by 7:00, I drove almost mechanically to a spot in a forest preserve I hadn't been to in 20 years. There he was, with a 20-year-old, caught in the act. Coincidence? I don't think so.

After that I daydreamed that I would be with a rugged, outdoorsy, construction type. Sure enough, the foreman of the company that remodeled our house heard I was separated and came over to tell me he always had a crush on me. Now we are engaged.

This is a case of a partly accidental manifestation. But one can use fantasies as a very powerful means of manifestation. We have already mentioned visualizations and the importance of "feeling" the end result of a desired outcome.

In a previous example, the person who desired a romantic relationship said that she "imagined what it would **feel like** to be in an ideal relationship." Instead of specifying every characteristic, she fantasized what it would be like when she was with that person in the present moment.

It was not a matter of creating a relationship in the future, because then you always manifest something in the future. She lived in her fantasy as if were real right now.

What was it like to spend time with him walking along the beach, sharing chores, raising a family, or being with each other's relatives? She not only pictured this but felt joy and happiness as if she actually experienced this.

She basked in the feelings, spending some time each day reliving them. This was also an enjoyable meditation in itself irrespective of when the actual relationship materialized. Look forward to visiting your fantasy story and trust that behind the scenes and out of consciousness, it is actually forming. Enjoy the fantasy time as an end in itself, as something you do for yourself.

Some people write about the desired relationship. A television documentary once showed a woman who created a story about falling in love with a dolphin trainer before she even had an aquatic job. At the time, this was a total fabrication, far removed from her present circumstances. She described the man's personality, appearance, and what interests they would share. Soon after, circumstances converted her fiction into physical reality.

This process is illustrated with examples and discussed further in the upcoming section called *Seeing the Goal Completed*.

Verbal Cues

Other participants put equal or greater emphasis on verbal cues. For example, one person spoke into a tape recorder saying, "An empty parking space is there when I arrive." Another person "thought" about her goal and recorded thoughts in a journal. "Generally, if I don't have time to visualize, I at least remember major manifestations at least once a day and review them in thought."

Affirmations are verbal statements, oral or written, that express a person's desire.

I didn't know how to start but I knew I had to do something. So I talked to myself, sometimes out loud and sometimes just in my head. I focused on what I wanted and allowed my intuition to formulate what to say. I would say things like, "I am excited and full of energy. I have the perfect job. I love my work." Some things didn't relate to what I wanted but I said them anyway. Things like, "I learn from my experiences. I love people and people love me. I am healthy."

———

Earlier in the year I needed additional income. When thinking about the kind of work I wanted, I saw myself working with children. I also wanted flexible hours and to enjoy what I was doing. After composing the general idea, I let go of it. Since I did not know exactly what I wanted, I didn't visualize. Instead, I affirmed every day for a week. I said, "I have a job that I can be creative in," and "I have a good time working."

Finally, at the end of the second week, Professor Fengler told us about a job available babysitting a five-month old. At that point I just knew this was the job I was supposed to have. I called the lady later that day and by the evening I had the job. I worked every Wednesday (my one free day) and she called if she needed me at other times. I am very happy and have no doubt that the job resulted from my affirmations.

Some participants used words in a prayer-like fashion. "While driving to work, I said, 'Day by day I am getting better.'" Another noted, "If I identify a specific goal, I say it out loud to someone and imagine how I will feel when I've achieved it." Many used both visual and verbal techniques.

One group member wanted to retire early. He created a "password" that represented the desire to leave his job.

> I didn't think my company would have another early retirement incentive because they recently offered one. It just wasn't in the cards, so I put together a package of how it would go. I needed a lot of energy since this was a big stretch of my beliefs. I used visualization and feeling. I visualized the specifics and felt the essence of the rest. I visualized the amount of pension I needed and that I would retire in one year. The rest focused on what it felt like to be retired. I would feel rested, joyous, full of energy, physically fit, and enthusiastic.
>
> Once I had this clear intention, I set up a symbol to remind myself to give energy to this manifestation. The symbol was a computer password that I used several times a day when logging in. When I keyed the word in, I savored the moment. I felt retirement; got a tingly sensation all over; and gave thanks as if it already had occurred. It took only a second or two. This not only energized my goal, but gave me a much more positive attitude during the day.
>
> I retired exactly one year later. I received more money than expected. I feel great and give thanks every day.

Words and the emotions they evoke are very powerful and it is important to be aware of them. Always state your desire in the affirmative. Remember where you direct your energy is what you attract. Instead of saying "I want to lose weight" or that "I don't want to be fat" say, "I am thin" or "I am at my perfect weight." Affirm it in the

present as if it has already occurred. Otherwise you emphasize the future.

By putting it in the future, you also avoid your present
state and what you resist persists. It is important to accept
where you are—in this case your present weight—before
you move to another state. Accepting yourself as you are
and desiring something new go hand in hand. Loving and
accepting yourself in the present is an important step to
successfully manifesting something new, a principle we
explore further in this chapter.

Our final example illustrates many themes. This person wrote that her "biggest wish for ten years or more was
to lose the weight I desired and maintain it easily." She
then listed the steps she took.

> In other areas I created what I wanted, but I
> was stuck on this one. Weight was a constant
> struggle in my life. First, I targeted the core
> belief, that I have a slow metabolism. I changed
> it to: "I have a super fast metabolism and my
> body converts everything I eat into pure health
> and energy." I loved saying that! I also affirmed
> that "It is easy to lose weight and hard to gain"
> since I understood that I had believed the op-
> posite.
>
> I created a simple picture of myself in a swim-
> suit surrounded by golden light. I refused to look
> at what "was." Each time the old image arose—
> after eating, looking in a mirror etc—I visual-
> ized the new one.
>
> I trusted myself completely with food, which was
> the first time since childhood. I ate consciously
> when I was hungry and stopped when I had
> enough, knowing I could have more when I was

hungry again. I switched to smaller meals more often.

I allowed no guilt, no matter what. If my body craved it, I affirmed that food was good, making me healthier and more beautiful. Without guilt and conflicts I enjoyed everything and smaller amounts satisfied me.

I complimented myself and saw myself as I chose to be. I thought about other enjoyable things the rest of the time. I switched my focus to love and appreciation of what I did want (my ideal weight) from hating and fearing what I did not want (gaining weight and being fat).

Within a few weeks I lost 15 pounds. Every day I appreciate my health and my body being able to take care of itself. Ever since I lost the weight 10 years ago, it has not been an issue.

This person illustrates several methods and procedures in a uniquely varied combination. This story proves that we can use multiple approaches with one manifestation. First, the subject recognized the beliefs needing deflation and those requiring affirmations and powering up. She transplants energy from unwittingly keeping an unhealthy weight to maintaining a vigorous and leaner body. She also created a swimsuit visualization to accompany the affirmations.

Notice how she trusts and accepts herself. She does not denigrate her body with feelings of hatred, rejection, and guilt. Rather than resisting the higher weight (and what we resist usually persists), she loves and trusts it to crave smaller servings.

Finally, she expresses appreciation for her health and body in the present and that serves as another kind of affirmation. Gratitude is a powerful and easily expressed method, yet we tend to overlook it.

Seeing the Goal Completed

Many participants visualized their goals in a completed state. One person used visualization to sell her home "by seeing myself at the house closing." Another created a "thought form of how it feels to have the goal already created. I put myself there, in it; I felt it and became it."

> Visualizing is a major component, since I am a very visual person. I see the family room addition as part of the house, just like I see myself at the ideal weight. But I also use written affirmations. I talk to myself silently and sometimes aloud.

> First I meditate and then visualize having my goal. Journal recording gives the needed energy and focus.

> I begin by writing out goals in detail, adding material over time. Out of this script I create a meditative visualization in which the goals already exist.

> I write goals down and reread them. Before sleeping or just when waking up, I mentally review them. I visualize moving through the situation from beginning to end.

One group member had a fairly detailed process. First, she states the importance of "becoming clear and definite about the goal." Second, she "writes it down, allowing room for even greater possibility." She thinks that becoming too focused or specific can limit outcomes and perhaps result in undesired consequences. Third, she meditates daily. During this meditation she "sees in detail, color, and form." She also feels with great emotion. During the day she also "affirms verbally whenever the opportunity occurs." Finally, she gives "heartfelt thanksgiving." Giving thanks for manifested desires is an act of self-love and builds confidence for subsequent goals.

Allowing It to Happen

You Have to Release the Arrow to Hit the Target

Clearly, we manifest all the time and our only choice is whether we wish to increase awareness and create more of what we want. Becoming alert to counterproductive beliefs and pinpointing any fear of failure are also important factors. If you want to manifest increased income but retain some belief that you don't deserve it, this perception sabotages a positive outcome. Based on a rational evaluation of present circumstances, you may think that money is impossible to create. This too will thwart your manifestations. So the first step is identifying the sources of resistance that may be interfering.

When attached to an outcome, we fear we are incapable of manifesting what we want. We may not trust our ability to manifest or perhaps the process itself. And a strong element of neediness emerges, usually associated with attachment. Neediness empowers the belief that we can't get what we want and that something must be wrong with us if we don't.

In a needy state, we must achieve the goal. Otherwise, failure substantiates our powerlessness or unworthiness. Without a certain object we may feel inadequate and incomplete. For example, if I don't marry, have children, a high-status job, or own a large home, I may see myself as a failure.

If I am not successful in creating a desired outcome, something terrible might happen, such as not supporting myself adequately, not having a place to live, or being the object of ridicule by peers and family. Perhaps I might disappoint someone who depended on me to be successful. Those I highly regard will no longer respect me. In the end, my failure to manifest proves once again that nothing ever goes right.

When attached to outcomes, we put a lot of energy on the fear of failure. For example, we may be manifesting more money while constantly worrying about its source. We always look for signs that our techniques are working and feel discouraged when we don't see immediate evidence of success. "If it's working, why don't I have more money?" we ask.

One participant planted peas but began to worry—after a week of colder-than-normal weather—when he couldn't see any sprouts. He dug down in one spot to reassure himself that some were sprouting. He did this day after day until only a few budding plants were left undisturbed. His patient neighbor had a full row of delicious peas to harvest.

You may desire a wonderful romantic relationship but not have much confidence in yourself. You may feel you don't deserve it or believe that—because you had bad luck in the past—you will likely attract a loser once again. We rerun these tapes and attract the same kinds of individuals over and over until we change how we think and feel about ourselves.

Sometimes we think we're detached, but doubt creeps in. Perhaps it takes the form of questioning the possibility of success, which is another way of saying "I am not sure I can be successful."

Admitting that part of you doubts dislodges the attachment. You no longer resist this fear while exploring ways of lessening the attachment.

Several examples that follow illustrate detaching, allowing, or even giving up. We need to trust the process. In a way trusting makes it easier on us. We don't have to figure it all out because the Universe does that for us. It seems that when we release our desire to the Universe without strings attached we can get back what we want effortlessly and sometimes even magically. We may even attract a much more elaborate version.

One man looked forward to a big hockey game with his sons. Tickets were on sale at the arena, which was in the same building where he was scheduled to play tennis that afternoon. He could pick up three tickets for that evening's game on the way to playing tennis.

> To my amazement and disappointment they sold out by the time I arrived. How could I go home and tell my sons this? Needless to say, I played terrible tennis and hurt my knee to boot. Near the end of the match I gave up and accepted the inevitable. I had done the best I could. Perhaps I was meant to do something else that evening, like go to a movie.

> On the way out of the arena, I stopped to see a former student—who was now the assistant hockey coach—to get some information. A few years back, he asked me for a graduate-school recommendation letter. I mentioned my inability to obtain tickets. He said he was sorry he hadn't known earlier because he gave his allotment of free tickets away.

> A few minutes later, he received a call from a friend saying he could not make the game. With

that, he reached inside his desk and pulled out three free tickets.

Here we see an almost magical timing of events. First, the assistant coach happened to be in his office when the man left the gym. Second, the coach just happened to receive that call during the ten minutes the man happened to be there. Finally, the number of tickets needed was three, the exact number returned to the coach.

The key to this occurred during the tennis match, when the man gave up and let go. This willingness to trust is not only challenging but also critical. We tend to hold on and measure progress. We must detach from the process and let it happen.

The next incident came from a reader of our first edition. Not only does her bagel story illustrate the importance of detachment, but it also demonstrates the need for flexibility about the outcome's form.

> In my newfound desire to make some big changes I happened to find your book. I was inspired by the stories and decided to really give it a try. I certainly had experiences of thinking of something and then getting it a short time after, but usually it was not very conscious.
>
> From the book's recommendation I decided to start with something simple, bagels. It's not unusual for someone to bring them to work but since no meetings were planned, it wasn't a given. I also hoped to manifest them in one day so it would be really clear and convincing. Well, I found myself putting a lot of energy out; more than I thought should be required for bagels.
>
> I kept thinking about bagels again and again and found myself getting discouraged by 9:30

when not a bagel was to be seen. At 10:30 I was frustrated because all my thinking about bagels had made me hungry. After 12, I finally let go. I thought, "Maybe tomorrow would be the day."

That evening my husband came home with pizza as he had planned, and—you guessed it—bagels. It just about blew me away. He very rarely brings home food from work. He told me that his secretary had thrust the leftover bagels into his hands as he was leaving. I think this little exercise impressed me as much as any spiritual lesson ever has. Quite amazing and so are the implications.

————

This morning I sat in my car waiting for the landlord to arrive to show me some apartments. I thought to myself, I hope one of these is it, but if it is not meant to be I can accept that. I was trying not to obsess or involve a lot of ego, which is tough when you desperately need to move and are looking for a place just for yourself.

I really wanted to be alone. I believe I didn't manifest this wish because I wanted it so much. I was really concerned about the outcome and was so obsessed about not manifesting what I wanted. I didn't get that particular apartment although later I did find a suitable one.

————

The prizes are always super, so I bought 12 raffle tickets and worked hard on visualizing winning first prize. I pushed and pushed and refused to just turn it over to the Universe. I did not win. As I reviewed this, I think I pushed too hard and wanted it too badly and tried to control, con-

trol, control. It doesn't work for me this way. It
seems the only way it works is to let go.

————

I want him to call so badly. I want this relationship and I want it now! I'm not very patient with
all this. I still let another person determine my
own happiness instead of creating my own. I
keep saying, "He's not calling. What's wrong with
me?" It is a control thing. I need to be happy
with me and know that the right man will come
along at the right time. However, when I do "let
go," he calls. When I feel needy he evidently picks
this up and backs off.

These examples illustrate the challenge of detaching and
letting go. For most people, detachment is not an issue
around parking places or small objects although anything
can become a prized item, as the bagel story illustrates.
The greatest challenge comes when the object is highly
desired or needed. Remember the man whose heart was
set on hockey tickets? He was attached because he waited
so long to pick up the tickets. He assumed that his sons
would be disappointed, and he would have let them down.
So his self-worth was at stake. The woman who wanted
her boyfriend to call felt needy and unloved. Her neediness
drove him away, which was the opposite of what she wanted.

It is not easy to say you don't really care if you get the
apartment or not when you are desperate to move and the
apartment seems perfect. To trust that your main desire
will be realized while the location and timing is out of your
hands can be trying. As one participant said, "I tried to
control, control, control."

Just as I got on the thruway a state policeman
pulled alongside going about 55 miles per hour.

No one wanted to pass. I felt increasingly anxious because if I didn't speed up I would be late. First, I tried to make him go faster. It was a forcing rather than a flowing. Then I said, "Screw it." I set a certain arrival time and just knew I would be punctual and relaxed. At that instant of relaxation the police car sped up to 70. It was instantaneous. I let it be okay to let whatever happens, happen. It was incredible!

———

I needed $100 for a trip to Hampton Beach within three days. I put it out and let it go. The whole process took only a few seconds. The next day my parents gave me an early birthday present. It was $100. I had said to the Universe I didn't care where it came from. I could almost feel it coming back to me. I didn't think about it. In previous years, I always got clothes plus maybe $25 or $50, but never more.

In these two situations, detaching brought the desired result. For the driver, forcing the situation was unsuccessful. He then just focused on the goal of arriving at a certain time and trusted that it would occur somehow. It was not a logical decision. For the birthday person, no thinking was involved; in fact, effort could have impeded this one. And she left the form entirely open, allowing many options instead of imposing restrictions.

In this culture, detaching from certain outcomes is often challenging, as the next two examples illustrate. The first is a game, an occasion with only one desired outcome in our competitive society—winning. We all grow up wanting to be champions at whatever we do. Few of us are content simply to do the best we can and enjoy the game itself. Yet detachment has relevance here.

> I was playing a former cribbage champion and kept getting all the good cards. I won all three games. I noticed she seemed hooked on winning. That much intensity puts out negative energy and keeps you from having it, which is the irony. Another time I was playing backgammon and didn't care about the outcome. I won the first two games! Then I really wanted to win the last game. My ego got involved and I felt the loss coming. When you must have something, you tighten up and it bites you.

We look at romance next, an area that often brings up many insecurities and doubts. In cultures with arranged marriages, romantic love exists outside of marriage, if at all, so ego is rarely involved. But in western society where our marketability as potential mates is paramount, ego and self-esteem influence dating situations. Why aren't we in a relationship? What's wrong with us? Does this indicate we are not desirable?

> In 1975 I realized my relationships weren't working, even some trial marriages. After so many attempts, I remember the frustration well. With a friend's help some time later, I realized I constantly forced it. I was putting out much energy and had to let the Universe take over. I gave up; let go; and said to myself, "Instead of making it happen I will let it happen." About a week later I met the woman who became my wife. Right away I was attracted to her. I allowed it to happen and consequently opened a space for it to occur.

Compare this last account with the woman who wanted her boyfriend to call and the subsequent frustration she created.

Detachment should not be underestimated, yet it can be an elusive concept. It does not mean that you don't have any desires or goals. Acceptance doesn't mean acquiescence. It means you aren't attached to the process itself. You trust that the results will manifest when the time is right and in an appropriate form. This is not the same as just hoping. It is even all right if it doesn't happen at all; perhaps something even better comes along later.

You might even go through the mental and visual process of what it would be like if what you want doesn't happen. Is it really all that bad and have you limited yourself to only one outcome? Fred, prepared once for a particular class all semester

> I was disappointed when it was cancelled. But I then had the opportunity to work on the revision of this book, which turned out to be equally satisfying and probably would not have been possible without that block of time away from teaching.

When you take energy off one very limited and specific outcome, you seem to free up the Universe to creatively formulate another of equal or even greater satisfaction. When you focus on a specific outcome, be mindful that it's just one of many fulfilling possibilities. This issue is discussed later in this chapter.

On some occasions your desire may not be appropriate, a situation that we explore later. This is why we recommend starting on desires with little emotional investment. When manifesting items of greater significance later, you will feel more confident and less attached.

Knowing, Intuition, and Reason

> I hadn't visualized a parking spot before I left but I knew I was going to find one.

> As soon as I got the phone call I knew I had the job. At the interview she said she still had other interviews scheduled and she would let me know but I knew I had it!

Again and again, participants used the word "knew" to explain part of the process. How did they know something was going to happen? In Chapter 2, how did the dance teacher know to put a sign on the front door so that the deliveryman could find her when she had no reason to suppose the costumes would arrive on that particular afternoon?

> A foot injury meant that I could not walk on it. After talking with you I sent some energy to see if I could heal it. At the time I went to bed I couldn't step on it without pain. The next morning when I got up I didn't even notice it, and realized it didn't hurt anymore. I **thoroughly believed** when I went to bed and woke up it wouldn't hurt anymore.

> We had only 40 minutes to travel a distance that usually takes a little over an hour. I couldn't pass on the thruway and traveled at less than the normal pace.
>
> After leaving the thruway everything went wrong. A car pulled out in front of us going 20 miles per hour. At that time I had a different feeling, like serenity or giving up. I had it clear in my head that we would be there at 7:50. Cars came and went. I don't know how or what the details are, but that is what will happen. I can just sit back. A logging truck pulled out in front

but I wasn't anxious. I didn't panic or try to pass
because I just **knew** we would be there on time.
The intersections took longer than normal.

I pulled into the parking lot and it was 7:50,
just as we knew it would be. It was an incredible experience! I have driven this route many
times, and know how long it takes. On the one
hand, we were surprised. On the other hand,
we weren't. It wasn't logic; it was just knowing.

Perhaps physicists would explain this experience with
space-time analysis. But logically, as the above individual
remarks, he couldn't explain how they covered that distance in such a short time. Even with speeding and no de-
lays from slow cars or long traffic lights, it would have been
impossible. And to arrive not only on time, but also at the
exact minute predicted is remarkable.

Yet many people have similar stories to tell. The only
necessary conditions seem to be a relaxed state of knowing
and being unaware of the time at any point during the trip.
This means not looking at a watch or listening to a radio.
Such knowing is an internal subjective awareness. Our society encourages observing external surroundings and ignoring our internal, intuitive environment. We are taught
that if something does not register with the five basic senses,
it is not real. Did it seem strange in Chapter 2 that "a little
voice" told the woman at the wine festival raffle to buy six
more tickets? Intuitive messages often contradict intellect
and reasoning; yet they are accurate and useful.

While picking up some fabric, I suddenly asked
the storeowner if she knew of any good uphol-
sterers. I had no idea why I asked except that I
have an antique chair I've thought about uphol-
stering for about 10 years but never had extra

money to do it. The next day I saw my mother,
who said she wanted to give me money to up-
holster the chair. Wow!

———

During my noon walk I thought, "I wonder what
I'll find that I need?" I kept walking and when I
reached the card shop, I realized I should go to
the bookstore. I found the perfect book there to
help with a personal problem I was wrestling
with.

Perhaps not surprisingly, women mention intuition more
often than men. Are we told as males not to trust anything
illogical or subjective in origin? If so, we can learn to augment
awareness of our own active intuition—those hunches that
often turn out to be inspired. The intuitive feeling is subtle.
Yet, as we have already seen, this subjective tool can be extremely valuable for manifesting. Besides giving useful information, it can help us avoid discomfort and disappointment.

I thought about taking some personal things
home, since we would be emptying the boat soon.
I thought I might need to take the dental floss. I
thought, "No, I have some at home." Well, when
I was cleaning my teeth tonight, the dental floss
ran out.

———

While unloading the car, my inner voice said I
should take the sun hat. My rational voice said,
"It's no good when it's really windy, and anyway,
I have a visor." Well, we had tremendous wind
gusts and within the first half hour my visor blew
off into the water. Today we spent about three
hours moving very slowly in the hot sun. I could
have used the sun hat. When will I ever listen?

I tried many times to reach a client with whom I had scheduled a session. As I got up to go to the bathroom I thought, "Wait. She'll call in a few minutes." I didn't wait. She did call and I was unable to speak to her.

I wanted a particular CD for months but didn't feel it was important enough to spend the money. So I stopped in a store to put up a poster for my course and my **inner voice** said, "Ask about the CD." The woman behind the counter said she ordered it for someone else but then returned it when the customer didn't buy it. I said, "Oh well" and took out my poster.

Suddenly she said, "Wait a minute." She dove under the counter and rummaged around. She promptly stood up with the CD in hand and said, "Here you can have it. It's a promo." So I got the CD I wanted and didn't spend a dime. I chuckled all the way back to the car.

It should be noted in the last example, that the manifestor not only tuned in to her inner voice but also detached when the saleswoman said she sent the CD back. That seemed to open up other possibilities. Not only does an inner voice communicate, but our bodies also send messages. Again, the answers can be very helpful if we overcome our cultural belief that only the mind should make major decisions. In the next example, a woman agonized over a job offer. Her mind encouraged her to take it, while her heart and body conveyed different messages.

I'm putting a lot of energy into making a logical decision. I asked the kids for their thoughts, and

I made a pros-and-cons list. I'm obsessed with finding the right answer. My body gives me the answer because I feel sick when I think about accepting the job, and a sense of relief when I consider turning it down. Instead of listening to my body, I justify the job because of the good pay, flexible hours, and convenient location.

When we run our lives using only logic, we limit and expose ourselves to unnecessary anguish. Notice that all the logical reasons for taking the job are responses to external expectations. She never mentions intrinsic satisfaction or fulfillment. When ignoring such useful cues from our body or intuition, we deny a part of ourselves. And in so doing we deny a richer and more joyful life.

Being Open to the Form It Comes In

A woman was caught in a flood. The water rose all around her house and she began to pray to the Lord to please come and rescue her. Soon after, the sheriff came by in a boat and asked her to hop in. She said she was waiting for the Lord to rescue her. So he went away and the water rose still further until she had to go to the second floor, so she prayed even harder. And soon a guy comes by on a log and asks her to hop on and she says "No." She is waiting for the Lord to rescue her. And now the water forces her to the roof and a helicopter comes by but once again she waves it off.

Soon after, the water washes her away and she ends up standing before God. She says, "Oh Lord I had such trust and you didn't save me!" And the Lord answers, "Lady, I sent you a boat, a log, and a helicopter. What else did you want me to do?"

This little story illustrates a very important concept: Be open to alternative ways for the Universe to satisfy our desire. The Universe often knows even better than we do the best means to fulfillment. Sometimes it delivers in wonderful ways we may have overlooked. At times it can be even more satisfying.

> It was the opening concert of the annual Mozart Festival. My mother, girlfriend, and I would soon be sharing this beautiful music together. Unfortunately, as we approached the tollbooth, I noticed a big sign saying, "Concert Sold Out." With great disappointment I pulled off to the side wondering what to do. My passengers were more disappointed for me than for themselves.

> It was a beautiful evening, and we drove into the mountains looking for a nice place to watch the sun set. Off one road I noticed a large gathering of cars. A passerby said the Vermont Symphony Orchestra was holding an outdoor concert. We walked to the entrance looking to buy tickets. Because we missed the opening number, the gatekeeper told us to forget the entrance fee. We strolled down to the front and had a wonderful free concert.

> Afterwards my mother took us to a nearby bar to buy us a drink. Within five minutes a pair of folksingers sang right in front of our table. We were entertained with a second free concert.

This man's heart was set on a concert that was sold out. However, his passenger's good will transferred to him. He gave up on the original goal and trusted they would have fun doing something together. In a word, he detached.

> I had no conscious awareness of the possibility of another concert. Yet, somehow, I was guided to that mountain road with the concert. My goal

was achieved. Only the form in which I had expected it to manifest was different. Through detaching from my original goal and form I was open to other possibilities of equal or even greater satisfaction.

Let's return to a previously discussed example to explore it in more detail. As this example illustrates, trying to control the form limits possibilities. For example, how could anyone forecast the following result?

> For over a year I wanted new colors in my living room studio. I researched the colors and patterns that would please and refresh me. It was a gradual process and I did not have the money for redecoration. However, in my imagination I visualized this change about twice a month. I had confidence that some day it would happen. I had no idea when but I knew the time for change was soon. I could taste it.
>
> One day a hose on my washing machine broke, flooding a good portion of the house, including the living room studio. An insurance check covered almost the entire cost of redecoration.

It would be hard to anticipate the "accident" that led to redecoration. Assuming one is honest, this is not something that one plans. Yet the goal was accomplished. Here is another example:

> I'm a good skier but I had never seen myself ski and wanted to. I was clear with my intent. I let it go and just knew it would somehow come to me. Perhaps someone would film me. For the next couple of days I looked for someone with a camera who would ski with me, but this did not happen.

The next time on the chairlift, my intuition told me to ski down a particular slope. I didn't want to do this because I just skied that one and wanted to try another slope while the snow was still good. I decided to listen to my intuition. It was cloudy, but as I skied the clouds opened up and the bright sun cast a perfect shadow directly in front of me just where I normally look. The shadow could not have been more perfectly placed! I could clearly see my style and this provided me the information I wanted. This incident taught me that we get what we ask for but not always in the form we expect.

In another incident the same person had a bad day shooting golf. His friend told him that a video would show him exactly what he was doing wrong. He "put it out" that he wanted to see himself playing golf and this included—but was not restricted to—a video recording.

That night he had a lucid split-screen dream, with two images side by side. On the left he saw himself with the wrong swing. On the right he saw the perfect swing and could easily see the difference. "I now knew what I was doing wrong. My shoulders were too tight." Once again this illustrates what happens when one does not limit possibilities. Who would expect the answer to come in a dream?

My husband wanted a computer but we didn't have the money. I said, "We'll manifest it." The next day he came home with a memo from the college saying they knew how important computers are to their faculty and that they were granting interest-free loans to purchase computers. This was totally out of the blue.

For years I wanted a nice warm fur hat that circles around the top of the head. Although this is a rather sad story, things do come to you even if you never know how. My husband's father died a couple of months ago. His wife gave me a hat like I just described. It means a lot because it was his. Again it proves things come to you but you don't know how or when.

After graduating, I was in a high-pressure job. After several months I did not know what to do except I knew I needed a break. Soon after, when I was out boating, I broke my big toe and had to limit activity for a whole week so it could heal.

My iron was completely plugged up. I could have thrown it out, but preferred to clean it, but how? I trusted an answer would come. On the way to bed that night I took a vitamin. On the medicine cabinet door was an article on how to clean things, including plugged-up irons. I was amazed but then said, "Of course."

I needed some Christmas paper to wrap my niece's gift but didn't have time to shop for it. There on top of the dumpster was some great wrapping paper. Things come to you when you want them.

As I was leaving class I thought of something I wanted to ask another student. I could see her in the far distance. I tried to imagine something happening so that I could catch up to her. She might slow down or maybe a rock would get in her shoe and she would stop to take it out. Nothing like that happened.

Later in the hallway, the girl walked right in front of me. This was the perfect opportunity to speak with her. This was even better than trying to catch up to her while she rushed home.

These stories did not involve extensive focusing, visualizations, or affirmations. Instead, the manifestations came from a certainty that an answer would materialize. The time from desire to result was sometimes quite lengthy, years in the case of the fur hat. In other instances, such as the dirty-iron account, the delay was brief. These participants **allowed** the process to bring the expected result. "Putting it out" was one phrase used. Also, most of them realized that everything does come, even though we can't forecast how.

One amusing incident concerns a car tape player. The button stuck and didn't eject the tape.

A group member and I decided on a joint miracle healing. We knew it was possible to "heal" mechanical objects. A few times a day, we visualized the apparatus working correctly. We had vivid visualizations, even seeing ourselves as little mechanics working on the release mechanism. For several weeks nothing happened.

While driving a friend home one day, I mentioned the problem and he just happened to have his tool kit. He took the tape recorder apart; squirted some oil on it; and it works quite well now. The whole process took 10 minutes. It was so easy compared to what my friend and I envisioned. This was a valuable lesson for both of us. By determining that scenario ahead of time we limited ourselves to just one possibility and made it far more complicated than was warranted.

This case again illustrates how we can limit ourselves by determining the outcome's form. In these instances, great abundance means that if we are not too attached to a specific form, we may actually receive something even more meaningful—or more easily—than expected. We may find that we get what we really want rather than what we think we want.

The next example points out the importance of having patience, openness, and trust in a process that eventually delivers our desire even if the way it happens is far beyond what we could imagine.

My dad and I looked at puppies because I really wanted a Boxer or Mastiff. We looked at Boxers one day at a breeder's home and found the exact one I wanted. She was adorable. The guy wanted $650 for her, so my dad told me to sleep on it. I thought about it all night and the next morning I knew I wanted her.

When we called the guy, he said she had already been sold that morning. I felt awful; I guess I couldn't let go and was too attached.

Soon after I had another chance. On Sunday one of my dad's old friends called and said that about eight weeks ago her Mastiff had puppies. She was wondering if we wanted to take a look. As soon as I saw them, I immediately fell in love with a female.

The connection was amazing and the lady even commented on it. The puppy's parents were top-prize-winning show dogs. The lady told my dad she was selling each puppy for $1,500. I wanted to cry because I did not have that kind of money. In fact I had none.

Later that day the lady told me she wanted to make a deal. She planned to keep one puppy to breed in a few years. She asked if I would raise and train the dog and then she would breed her. She would then sell those puppies. After that breeding, I would keep her and decide whether or not to breed again. The dog was mine! We brought her home and everyone loves her.

I am convinced of two things. First, I let myself detach long enough to let the Universe work with me. Also, maybe the first puppy was not right for me. This puppy and I are definitely connected. If I got the other dog, who knows if we would have bonded? I firmly believe the right thing happened!

The final example involves a teacher who wanted to win a special teaching award.

I so wanted to win. I didn't get it, but I received a call from the professor who evaluated my presentation for the award. He introduced himself as the person who had the pleasure of sitting in my class. He said I made such a tremendous impact on him.

My talk was on death, dying, and grief. His sister-in-law was dealing with her father's death, and he wanted to know how to help her. This was a wonderful affirmation of my attempt to teach students how to cope with loss. I realized I had not failed to be effective. I was able to let go of my sense of failure. I don't need to win an award to know that my teaching does make a difference.

Gratitude

One of the most powerful and easily overlooked forms of manifesting is being grateful for what you already have, particularly something you love. When you get that last parking place, unexpected money, or a clean bill of health, thank the Universe. Gratitude conveys the message that you want more of the same. You attract what you focus on. If you put energy on affirming your pleasure with the desired outcome you will likely attract more of the same or something similar. Thoughts have energy and gratitude manifests more of what you desire.

You don't even have to wait until you manifest something to be grateful. You can be thankful even before you experience it. Gratitude now for a future manifestation indicates trust and confidence. After all, how can you appreciate the presence of something you don't already have now, unless you completely trust in its eventual materialization? Gratitude ahead of time actually empowers and enhances its creation.

Unfortunately in this culture, we emphasize problems but rarely appreciate solutions. After something is resolved we immediately concentrate on another problem. Once we attain a goal, we find something else lacking and try to manifest that without expressing thankfulness for this success.

Appreciate what you have while also placing attention on your desires. Spend some time putting thoughts and energy on things you can savor about yourself and your life.

This final example illustrates many principles we have already discussed including trusting, allowing, being open to the form it comes in, and believing in abundance.

If I need money I just put out to the Universe that I need money. I always say, "I need at least this much." That leaves it open for the Universe to give me more.

Recently I needed to pay off my student loan. I thought the money could come as a new client, or a gift from my grandmother. It might even come from my grandfather's estate or some other direction. So I set my intention. It never takes much effort and it always happens. Whenever I turned my computer on I set my intention to have at least enough money to pay off my student loan.

About a week later a big hailstorm made a few dents in our aging auto. The insurance company gave us $7000 to get it fixed or replaced. We didn't care about a few dents so we used the money to pay off the loan.

I always release it to the Universe and trust it will come. When I feel I don't have enough, I always give some money away. That affirms my belief in an abundant Universe. That's why I constantly give. I believe the Universe works this way.

As we close, let's briefly review elements for successful manifestations. First, develop clarity in your goals. Second, choose a comfortable method. Third, after doing the technique, release or detach from the outcome. Fourth, allow it to manifest and don't try to force it. Fifth, trust that what is highest and best for you is now in the works.

For many of us, controlling everything is an appealing rational approach. We want to direct both the unfolding and final result, but many anecdotes highlight drawbacks and limitations to such rigidity. Conversely, trusting the Universe's broader perspective produces definite benefits. A greater range of options and opportunities can present themselves. Wonderful little surprises can greet us, with better outcomes than those we would have commandeered.

Finally, gratitude is a powerful but often overlooked method. When we are grateful for something positive we recognize the Universe's abundance while also affirming that more of this be sent our way. For example, appreciating the warmth and encouragement of a supportive friend attracts more of the same from those around you.

This is a very important chapter, packed with information. To make it easier to remember the main points we present them in summary form below.

Basic Principles of Manifesting

Be clear on your intention

Decide what you want and concentrate on the desired results. Resist focusing on the solution. Let the Universe take care of the details.

Power-up your Creation

Visualize what it is like to experience your desire, by using all five senses. By combining sight, smell, sound, taste, and touch, the visualization is real in your imagination. In so doing, it becomes embedded in the subconscious as part of your reality.

Affirmations or other techniques are most effective when stated in the present tense. For example, "I now have a wonderful job." Avoid affirming in the future, such as, "I am going to have a wonderful job" because then the results will always be pending.

Be positive. Affirm what you do want, rather than what you do not want. For example, "I don't want to be alone" is a negative statement. Rather, affirm: "I'm now with someone wonderful who enjoys being with me". This statement is much more powerful and reinforcing.

Emotions energize manifestations. Experience how it feels to have what you want. Are you happy, dancing with joy, or feeling good all over? Get involved and be passionate.

Allow it to happen

Trust the process. We tend to want a progress report to check if it is working. However, if we dig up the seed to see if it is growing, we never get the flower.

Beliefs are self-fulfilling. If you believe you can manifest something, then your manifestation happens easily. The more you believe you can't, the harder it gets. Start out easy and work up to difficult goals. You fortify your belief with each success.

Be open to the form. The Universe indeed works in mysterious ways and is much more creative than we could ever be. Sometimes we miss it altogether. Put your intellect on hold and let your intuition be your guide.

Detach from the results. Attachment or "neediness" comes from fear or a belief that you can't create what you want. Move the energy from fear of not getting to accepting what you do get. Acceptance opens the space to allow goals to manifest.

Gratitude fertilizes the soil and prepares it for better plants to grow. Small blessings grow into larger ones. Praise and thanksgiving substantially increase spiritual power.

Remember that manifestation is just one more tool supplementing a more active and familiar repertoire. The person who wanted his roof fixed in the opening chapter could have sought out competent workmen as well as waiting for one to knock on his front door.

Working with one's beliefs is more effective than dealing with resistance generated by the unfamiliar. If you believe strongly in action over meditative or passive methods, then active ways may make more sense. You can always supplement with imagery, fantasy, or other complementary additions.

We again close by encouraging you to experiment. If one recommendation does not seem right, try something else. So many ways to successful manifestation exist, that no single approach emerges as the best. Even the many people we were privileged to work with and heard from over the past ten years have not represented all possibilities. Above all, learn to listen to that inner sense; follow it; and allow it to happen.

Chapter 4

When the Energy Flows

In the first three chapters, we discussed a variety of successful short-term manifestations, such as parking places, enjoyable experiences, and desired objects. We presented glimpses of larger and more elaborate manifestations to illustrate detachment and trust. In this chapter we focus on only one person's manifestation. The desired goal grows out of a series of issues most of us have asked ourselves at some point. What is our real life's work? Do we deserve a job that uses our talents and creative skills while financially supporting us? Can a job bring us greater satisfaction than our present situation and do we have the courage to go for it?

This is the story of a woman who, at first, felt she had to settle for a job she hated simply to support herself. However, within a short time there she found a way to do what she loved and be paid for it. She wanted to attract a job that would use her special talents and give greater satisfaction.

This account includes many of the concepts and techniques we have already discussed. It also introduces material we explore later in the book.

The first section is a transcription of her account. The second portion discusses parts of her story, highlighting the particularly relevant aspects. When you have reached that point, we encourage you to reread the account, appreciating its detail and significance. This remarkable example shows what's possible when you define a goal clearly and commit yourself to achieving it.

Manifesting the Perfect Job

I started work as a bookkeeper because I desperately needed an income. I was out of work for six months and my personal life was not good. I was coming from a very scarce place in my life. I took the first job offered. I had no accounting background and no desire to be a bookkeeper.

I did the work adequately, but my best skills were not being used. The job was not only drudgery, but it also gave me no joy. I went to work every day and did what I had to do. I was uncomfortable because every day I punched numbers into the computer. I hated it for the 18 months I was there. Three months into it I knew I needed something else but how could I go about finding it?

Finally I had to do something. For quite awhile, I read the classifieds and attended functions that might help, but nothing happened. I realize now that bookkeeping was not why I was there.

Fortunately, while I was on the job, a lot of healing was going on. I gradually built self-esteem, which at the time was really low. That came from working with people who liked me as a person and did not identify me with the job.

I got involved with a lot of creative things there and energy really started to flow. During my time off, I made jewelry and hosted shows. The organization was designing a new building to move into and asked me to be the interior designer. I was doing a lot of things unrelated to my job and it was having a positive impact on my self-esteem.

Eventually, I was emotionally ready to visualize what could come next. I began affirmations about three months before I left the company. While walking to work, I talked to myself and stated aloud what I wanted. I said, "I deserve to be loved," "I am loveable," "I am bright and intelligent" and "I need to be at a job using my skills."

I didn't think a lot about it. I just said whatever I needed to say. I reminded myself by writing affirmations on a chalkboard attached to my apartment door, so when I left, I could remember them. These included, "Abundance" or "Keep breathing," in times when I felt tight.

For a couple of months, I recited these affirmations daily for about 15 minutes on my way to work. People looked at me strangely because I was talking to myself. This made me smile. Going to work was a visualization exercise for the future, a sort of affirmation for the positive things in my life now and for those on the way. Coming home after work, I released the day's stress and negativity. Sometimes I felt bad about myself, or the job, and wanted to shake it off.

I didn't have a specific job in mind, but I did have some thoughts and feelings about it. I wanted some autonomy and to use my communication and organizational skills. I also hoped that things would come more easily.

Most of my life I had chosen things where I had to work really hard and struggle. I was not interested in doing that any longer. I wanted to find a good fit. All my life, people would tell me, "You are so good at talking to people," and "You are incredibly articulate and sensitive." These compliments neither helped me feel secure nor created a real level of abundance.

I didn't know what to visualize or what job to ask for. I kept affirming, "I find something suitable using these skills. I don't know right now what that looks like and what the job name is, but I want to do that."

I also had a time limit because the organization was moving. I knew I was not going with them because of transportation problems. I did not own a car and couldn't afford one. Though I felt no sense of urgency, I knew I had a deadline. It had to happen sooner than later and the time restriction worked well. In my heart of hearts I knew it would happen. I didn't know if it would be the perfect thing but I knew something would come along.

I started applying for positions and going for interviews but things weren't clicking terribly well. I saw one ad I liked but I lacked the qualifications. So I didn't apply because I didn't have the confidence and feared that I would fail to get it. A friend of mine said I would be perfect for this job. "I know the woman and she is really nice. Talk to her and get your foot in the door," she said.

So I made the phone call and, by chance, two women had the same last name and I got the wrong one. She was cold, rude, and had no idea what I was talking about. I called my friend and she told me to try again, but I really didn't want to. I was resisting the whole process.

I didn't want to get my hopes up because I would be disappointed. But my friend encouraged me to call again and I did. This time I reached her, but she was on her way out and was brief and not very friendly. So I decided not to apply, let it go, and did not think about it again.

About a week later on a Sunday morning, I was with my friend at a laundromat I never go to. The program director was there so my friend said, "That's her. Let me introduce you." We met over some washing machines. She was in her raggedy clothes and so was I.

We talked about a lot of different things and I asked her to tell me about the job. I knew by her description that I could do it. But I didn't have the skills on paper. She asked if I had applied for the job and I said no. She encouraged me to apply and seemed to like me. That gave me more confidence, so I wrote a cover letter, which had to be on her desk the next day. Usually when I do cover letters it takes days to write them, but I had it there by noon the next day.

Now that she has it, let it happen. She has since told me that had she just seen my resume, she probably would not have called because I did not have the appropriate qualifications. Meeting me made a big difference.

During the interview, we enjoyed a natural and easy connection. It was just "meant to be," though I hate to use that cliché. She told me I was one of three finalists, but they were strongly leaning towards this other woman. So I thought, "Well, I will go through this exercise for the practice, but I probably won't get the job." When I went into the interview—and I have never done this before—I acted as if I already had the job. I basically presented my agenda for that position.

I let go of my expectations. I decided I was just going to be myself and be creative. I didn't care what they thought because I am not that invested in it anyway. Because I let it go, my confidence level was up and it felt right. It was easy and I felt comfortable, so everything moved. They were so impressed they offered me the job on the spot. They never even finished the other interviews.

I remember thinking, "I don't believe it; this pays $10,000 more than the job I have now." I knew I needed more than I was making, but I wasn't attached to the money and thought I would get salary increases in stages. Making that kind of money in a chunk surprised me and it was not so difficult. They hardly asked me any questions. It just fit and we all felt it.

The job has just been incredible. I have autonomy as well as a lot of responsibility. I constantly use my creative skills. I attend meetings, talk to people, organizing events, and hire and supervise employees. I'm doing everything I've always wanted to do. Because I love it, I'm doing a great job.

Three months into it, management upgraded the position because I am doing more and working at a higher level than expected. I like when they tell me I am doing a great job and to keep it up. "What can we do to help you?" they keep asking. It is empowering. In most of my former jobs I heavily advocated for raises and recognition. It was a real struggle. In this job, I receive more affirmations than I can deal with some days. Sometimes I can barely stand to hear one more compliment, yet it helps me work more effectively.

It just feels like it was meant to be. Affirming that it was going to happen helped to prepare for and recognize it. I trusted that the Universe would provide. I gave it some clear direction as to what I wanted and then stepped back and let it happen.

Many times opportunities arise and you try to make it happen, though you kind of hold on to something. You say to yourself that this has to work. I had to get out of my own way and take my best shot. Then let everything else fall into place and trust it would work. I let go and it worked for me.

Manifesting a Car

This story has an interesting sideline. One reason this woman had to leave the first organization before they moved was that she did not have a car. However, her new job required her to travel around the state; thus she would have an even greater need for a vehicle. She had very little time and almost no money to buy one. Once again, her personal account is both informative and inspirational.

I sold my car to travel 10 years ago. Since then, I never had enough money for even a down payment. I have always had to depend on others for transportation.

So when the organization moved, I knew I would not have a job because I could not get to the new location. If everything would fall into place, I needed to help it along.

I decided to do a jewelry show to raise money. I had $1,500 in mind, but thought that was too much to ask for. Maybe I could raise $1,000. That would be okay, but $1,500 was in the back of my mind.

For about three or four months I made jewelry in my spare time. For a big show, I needed 200 to 250 pieces, but I knew that was absurd. After a month I had ten pieces. I really had to work hard and felt stressed out. I work well under pressure, so I just pumped them out.

About a week before the show I sat down to count the pieces and I had 250. Before this, I had no idea how many I had. So I invited 100 people and about 80 came. People brought gifts and flowers and we had food and dancing. Customers bought jewelry as if the pieces were on sale. I spent the whole time talking and wrapping. I never left the room because they were buying like crazy. This was a wonderful testament to my artwork and a real demonstration of support and friendship from the community.

The show surpassed the vision of what I wanted. People were so loving towards me. It was a full day and I was exhausted. I was so burnt out for days after the show that I didn't count the money. After a few days, I realized I made $1,500 to the penny. During the sale I didn't even think about the amount. I was just in the moment, selling things like crazy.

A week later I put a down payment on a car. The timing was perfect. They wouldn't have given me the job if I didn't have a car. I got the job before my show, and it was an act of faith that I would have enough money for a car. I told them I was buying one, but I didn't know how at that time. I was hoping the show would provide that for me. I knew the job would pay enough to cover car payments. It all happened at the same time. The car came one week before I started the job.

Again, letting go and trusting made it happen. I gave it my best shot and then stepped back.

So I have a car and a job I love. I'm making more money now than I had in 15 years. It was not only easy, but it also keeps building on itself.

It's really interesting how energy works. I feel good about what I do and positive about myself. So people respond differently. Now when I tell people what I do, it feels like a truer representation of who I am. I feel good about who I am in the world. Everything starts to flow.

When you do what's right, it clicks and fits into place. It is not that you don't have challenges, but you have the tools to meet them. I have a lot more faith in abundance and that things really can happen. A certain bit of magic is at work. I don't know how we create it or how the Universe creates it for us, but it is wonderful.

Here I am driving through southern Vermont with the beautiful snow on the mountains. I'm in my new car listening to classical music and saying to myself, "I get paid to do this. I get paid to talk to people and drive in this beautiful countryside." I don't punch a clock. When I meet people, they pick up on the positive energy. It is almost as if the words don't matter. I'm happy doing what I do. I believe in the program and I'm so comfortable that people want to be a part of it. They ask, "What can we do? How can we make this work?" If I approached them bummed out, maybe they wouldn't want to be part of the program regardless of how they themselves felt. It is amazing how positive energy creates more and more positive energy. It works upon itself.

Commentary on Manifesting the Perfect Job

This is a very human story. Though it has a happy ending, this woman experienced considerable self-doubt and fear at various points. She literally hated her bookkeeping job. When we really hurt, a way out is hard to see. Everything often goes wrong at the same time. A significant personal relationship just broke up; she was out of work for six months; and all she could find was "real drudgery." She recognized she was coming from a "scarce place." However, beggars can't be choosers. The pain finally got to the point where she "had to do something" but she didn't know what. How often it is that things have to get really bad before we take corrective action! We even tolerate a bad work situation when we fear the alternatives. Better the unpleasantness of the known than the risk of the unknown, even if great rewards await us.

It is worth noting that she did take advantage of available resources. Her world was not one of total scarcity. She identified with colleagues who supported her. She also immersed herself in creative activities that had nothing to do with her job, but were helpful in building self-esteem.

She also began a series of regular affirmations. The regularity and commitment to the process was more important than the particular wording. She said whatever she "needed to say that day." It could have been anything needed at that moment—anything! She was in charge and worked from a point of present time. She did not "think a lot about it" and simply worked the routine into her daily life. She said out loud to herself what she wanted rather than only asking for what she thought was realistic.

She talked positively on the way to work and was not particularly concerned about what others thought of her. Coming home was "a sort of letting go" of the "pain, stress and negativity" she experienced on the job. She forgave herself for the work situation and didn't indulge in a victim mindset. It would have been so easy to fall into the "poor-little-me" consciousness. But by releasing the stress on her way home, she was open to creating a new, more supportive environment. So often we remain mentally mired in negative circumstances and do not fully free ourselves to commit to and create a new situation.

Note that she "didn't have a specific job in mind for the visualization," though she "did have some thoughts and feelings about it." She knew that certain attributes should be included in any job, such as a feeling of autonomy and the use of her communication skills. She wanted a "fit" between the needs of the job and the personal skills she felt she could bring to it. A job had to be more than just a paycheck. She wanted to be paid and supported for doing what she loved.

"Knowing" was also part of this manifestation. "I came to the realization it would happen," she says. "In my heart of hearts I knew it." She wasn't relocating with the organization and "knew something would come."

At this point, trust and detachment were paramount. She had not identified a specific job; all she had were "thoughts and feelings" about it. Consequently, she transmitted her desire to the Universe and then watched for the unfolding. On the surface, it looked like the manifestation was not even working. She got mixed up and called the wrong person. Then she decided to not even apply for the job. She "**let it go** and did not think about it again." As she learned later, had she submitted her resume to the director at the start, she likely would have been rejected because she didn't have the appropriate qualifications. We can never forecast the best unfolding of events.

Who could have anticipated a chance meeting at a laundromat she never went to? This was a crucial introduction, since her resume was weak. Was this really a chance meeting? We leave that to the reader's speculation.

During several phases of the interview process, notice how frequently she refers to "letting it go." After she left her resume on the director's desk, she "let it go." During the interview she decided to be herself and not "care what they think because I wasn't that invested in it. I let go of my expectations," she says.

In detaching, her attitude was that she didn't need the job. Neediness can actually get in the way. By viewing the interview as an "exercise for practice" and pretending she already had the job, she circumvented attachment. Learning what "tricks" work best can be extremely helpful, particularly in an emotionally charged situation, such as a job interview. By having to win you might actually increase the chances of losing.

When she held the jewelry sale, she says, "During the sale I didn't even think about the amount . . . I was just in the moment." Even after the show "for days I didn't count the money." As she says, "I let go and trusted it was going to happen."

Finally, "When you feel good about yourself, everything starts to flow," she said. Situations and experiences fall into place effortlessly. In turn, her energy brings more creative opportunities and others "pick up" on it. "It is almost as if words don't matter." People sense her positive energy and want to become a part of that, which in turn promotes her work goals as well as their own. Her energy and enthusiasm are amplified and mirrored by others. This creates further productivity and satisfaction for her and probably everyone involved.

She doesn't understand how it all operates, but it isn't really necessary to comprehend the process to know that it does work. "A certain bit of magic kicks in. I don't know how we create it or how the Universe creates it for us. But it is wonderful!"

Chapter 5

Why We Don't Always Manifest What We Desire

One group member, Ed, was on vacation in Florida with his friend Jim. They shared a love for golf and played several times a week. One day they paired up with another man and his wife. Jim introduced himself with: "Hi, I'm not that good of a golfer and I always hit the ball in the water. By the way my name is Jim."

Ed thought that was a strange introduction. "I thought that Jim is going to lose a lot of golf balls because this course has a lot of water."

Indeed, on the very first hole Jim drove the ball right into the pond and announced, "I always put the ball into the water." Ed tried to keep from smiling. "I really had to restrain myself because I wasn't surprised at all. He was an excellent manifestor."

Unfortunately, the game really slowed down. According to the rules, if you hit the ball into water you have to drop a new ball just on the side where it entered. That meant Jim still had to hit it over the pond but this was a much easier shot because he was right at the water's edge instead of back where he teed off.

Though it was a short shot, the ball again sunk into the pond. Finally, after the third attempt and to speed things along a little, Ed said it was all right to place the ball on the other side so he didn't have to hit over any more water.

Well, this happened for every hole thereafter. It was like a ritual. Just before he teed off he announced, "I always hit shots into the water;" the ball always obeyed; and Jim felt terrible. With each hole his frustration mounted.

"I was very interested in what would happen on the one hole that did not have water. Maybe he would hit the ball out of bounds. Jim took a bigger than normal swing knowing water was not a problem. He hit the ball on the toe of the club (instead of in the middle) and the ball shot out 90 degrees away from its intended direction. Much to his surprise and Ed's amazement the ball went into a pond at the 17th fairway. Jim finished the last two holes the same way he played the whole day. The ball never touched down on dry land.

The more Jim played, the more dejected and frustrated he got. From a different perspective, Ed could see that Jim was totally successful because the ball reached water, just as he announced beforehand. What a great example of how fear, frustration, and affirmation can combine to create a perfect manifestation."

In another instance, a man and his wife visited the fairgrounds with a friend from New York. While eating at a picnic table, the friend noticed seagulls circling overhead. "I hate seagulls," she remarked. "I'm always afraid they're going to poop on me." Less than a minute later, a large load landed in her hair. A few days later, this same woman was back in New York jogging. Within a few minutes a seagull dropped a load, hitting her squarely in the chest.

Surely she didn't desire either experience. In fact, she wasn't even consciously thinking about seagulls the second time. Yet in some way she attracted both experiences.

As we've clearly seen, our beliefs constantly create outward reflections in the physical world, and no external censor says, "Oh, she doesn't really mean or want this." What we experience in physical form is exactly what we expect or believe.

What Belief Creates an Undesirable Manifestation?

To ask this presupposes that we willingly accept responsibility for unpleasant experiences, such as being bombed by seagulls. It is much easier to blame the birds, a cruel act of fate or, if all else fails, the government for not getting rid of the dirty nuisances.

Perhaps we don't immediately recognize how a belief could be manifested in bird droppings. How does the principle of continuous manifesting explain that I haven't won Megabucks yet, that I haven't found the perfect mate or job, and that my health could stand much improvement? Some days I don't get a convenient parking place when I definitely need one and I consciously desire other things. Yet our experiences (or projections) do not always seem to match our desires. We all have times when it seems hard to manifest anything and our lives appear to be caught up in a whirlwind of events that seem out of our control.

This chapter examines some of the bigger challenges recounted in our workshops. Working effectively was not always simple. It was a learning experience that included frustration and even some perceived failures.

Yet few group members found these disappointments totally discouraging. In fact, greater learning and enjoyment often came from our so-called failures than from successes.

Our Unrecognized Beliefs Around Scarcity

We begin with a mundane incident that all of us have probably experienced at some point. Yet, this example illustrates many principles that can help us understand why we might not manifest some larger desires.

> It was one of those days when I did not have enough time for everything I needed to do. Everything came up at once. Just when I had things lined up, my wife gave me four more things to do. She kept telling me to hurry because we had so much to do.
>
> So I started with some errands. I was on the road for a few minutes when this little old man pulled out in front going two miles an hour and I couldn't pass him. The light was green but he slowed down so it turned red. I became more and more frustrated. But then I sat on the sideline and watched the frustration instead of letting it run me.
>
> I took the position of an observer. As I drove along, all I did was watch. I never saw so many hindrances going from point A to point B. Just as the old man pulled into a gas station, this big dump truck pulled out in front. The intersection was backed up three lights' worth as I watched this all unfold.
>
> I ended up an hour late and could have walked faster. I began to recognize that I believed in the scarcity of time. It was a lesson plan in disguise and I flowed with the energy. I was fascinated to watch and see what happened.

Getting more and more frustrated and angry or blaming some external source would have been easy. He had plenty of choices: the little old man, the dump truck driver, his wife, God, or even the authorities, who did not provide a four-lane highway and synchronized traffic lights.

However, this man knew that everything referred to some belief. He accepted responsibility for this frustrating series of events (perhaps reluctantly) and sought the belief behind the manifestation. He looked to his own experience for the lesson. By simply observing his own experience, he worked back to the belief creating the experience. By becoming fascinated with events as they unfolded—and by not judging them—he identified it. Thus, he ultimately gave himself the choice to change that belief, or at least give it less power. On that particular day he strongly believed in the scarcity of time.

Simply retaining a belief does not lead to manifestation but rather the energy we give it. Worry and frustration animated this man's concept of time scarcity. Over and over he said, "There is not enough time." Like the good mirror that life is, his experiences reflected that belief.

To have the choice of changing a belief—or the amount of energy placed on it—first identify the kind of belief that might create such circumstances. This requires taking responsibility for one's circumstances and often a bit of detective work. As open-minded investigators, we more easily discover causal beliefs in a nonjudgmental atmosphere of open and honest searching.

Here's another example: For several years, a manifestor enjoyed excellent health all winter but then came down with a serious cold in early spring. "When I realized I created this in response to believing it is not normal to go through an entire winter without at least one cold, I was able to break that unpleasant cycle."

Assuming responsibility for his spring cold helped him to recognize various sources for his beliefs. Everyone around him seemed to get at least one winter cold. What made him different? Fear set himself up for a disabling cold when it finally did come.

> I felt I had used up some imaginary and unspecified amount of good health, which I would have to pay for at some time in the coming year. I had to deal with a specific belief in scarcity of good health as well as a more general belief that I must earn or balance some good experiences with some not-so-good ones.

> Though my father passed away many years earlier, I could still hear his voice: "Into every life some rain must fall," and "Experiencing hardship builds character."

One group member felt that recording desires was a counterproductive form of bragging. "It makes me feel like I am boasting and saying, 'Look what I can do.' Perhaps just staying in awe of manifestations is a respectful place to be." She thinks that in our culture it is not okay to be prosperous and also feel good about it. On the one hand, if a strong, persistent perception dictates scarcity as the norm, then it may be inappropriate to want too much. On the other hand, if one lives in a perceptible world of abundance, then we can all celebrate good fortune.

Several participants dealt with a lack of work or money. One manifestor felt "harried and desperate about money." He was, "Doing work I dislike and I don't know how to change it. I have a lot of fear." He was afraid to leave a job he detested and that paid poorly; yet he made no effort to project a new goal. "I think I've avoided setting meaningful goals to avoid disappointment. Without a goal, I avoid obstacles to achieving it. Nothing ventured, nothing lost."

Not only did he subscribe to a belief in scarcity of meaningful and more lucrative work, but he also lacked a belief in himself to manifest a suitable job. His own fears about past failures and the current poor economic conditions almost paralyzed him. Yet, he was also aware that he could choose to move beyond self-doubts, fears, and limiting beliefs.

It is so difficult to trust that I can pay bills if I go after a job that really turns me on. I struggle to let go of fear and the assumption that we have to do what we don't want or believe in to survive. We know deep down this is not true, yet our fears and culture overrule our heart and spirit. I know it is time to trust that more.

A part of him, what he defined as his "heart and spirit," was leading him more and more in the direction of trusting in himself and the Universe's abundance.

Several months later he formulated some answers. "We can become more conscious and make friends with our fears. We can listen instead of running away." He recognized that, "Changing beliefs is a slow process because we essentially change who we are. It takes practice to be a good tennis player, so expecting immediate results only creates frustration. Why not enjoy the process?"

By focusing on lack, we attract more of what we do not have. We hold onto present circumstances—such as a job we detest—because we don't believe in a natural abundance to provide suitable things at appropriate times. Believing that we must struggle to attain desired things may also imply a belief in scarcity. In other words, if we thought those desired things are abundant, we would more likely believe that they are also easily accessible.

It is a challenge not to be affected by the environment. If the media constantly reminds us of adversity for others or warns of bad times ahead, we often internalize those beliefs and thus manifest them.

> We hear more and more about the national economic slump. As a self-employed street artist, I'm easily stressed and it's difficult not to worry. I have a hard time foreseeing financial success when the people and papers claim economic problems.

> I know my fear of tight wallets causes me more trouble than the actual economy itself. And I recognize that if work stays slow it could prove that I need to move on or change. Realizing I could cause my own lack of customers got me to focus on reversing that. I have allowed whatever happens to unfold, feeling secure enough even if it stays slow. To my delight, these past few days have brought business galore. It feels like tourist season.

This statement illustrates several things. First, this person accepts responsibility for his own circumstances. Though society is plagued by an economic turndown, his belief in alternatives could make his business an exception to the rule.

Second, he's willing to move to a new job or location if conditions do not improve. He is open to new avenues through which abundance can be manifested. Finally, he allows, "Whatever happens to unfold," trusting that an appropriate experience follows. Many of us in similar situations worry, obsess, and want to control circumstances with our livelihood at stake. He **detached** and allowed for abundance.

Attachment Is Believing You Cannot Create What You Want

It seems cruel that just when we most need or want something, we actually create the opposite. A strong feeling of neediness keeps good from us.

At the end of the first year, we sent out a questionnaire, asking participants which factors facilitated manifestations and which detracted. A common observation was that detachment and confidence were important facilitators. Feeling "needy" and "having to be in control" were inhibitors.

> I was most successful when I was open to the outcome and didn't have a preconceived idea. I had the most trouble manifesting when I desperately wanted; thought I knew what I wanted, or what the outcome should be. When I feel busy and need it the most is when I don't seem able to manifest.

> I'm least powerful when I'm attached and feeling I just have to have it! At that time I'm coming from a place of insecurity and fear.

> I'm most powerful when I feel good about myself, relaxed, playful, and loving. Then I can let go and allow the Universe to take care of it. I have difficulty when I am depressed, feeling out of control, angry, or need to control people and situations

> My greatest successes materialize when I feel strong and confident and when the desired element isn't desperately needed.

> Common prerequisites for my failures included stress and lacking confidence in the intended

result. After noting that disbelief or discouragement paved the way to letdown, I concluded that
playfulness and confidence (not arrogance)
brought me success.

————

I'm also new to manifesting and now see it would
take some time to get comfortable. I can quickly
become impatient with something new. I need
to enjoy learning something rather than becoming distressed because I don't manifest everything after three weeks. The first time a manifestation didn't work out I immediately doubted
the process. I look back and see how impatient I
was. I wanted amazing and immediate results,
but I now see that learning something new takes
time and patience.

The last story raises an important point: It takes some
time to get used to this, to feel comfortable about creating
one's reality. The street artist noted that when he worried
and felt needy was when he had difficulty making sales.
He added, "When I start the day slowly, I lose all confidence in myself and the possibility for having a good day.
Believing that I am a good artist and not thinking about
the need to make money seems to lead to more sales."

An art teacher and a practicing painter noted, "It is important to be energetically connected to my art as expression and not as a money maker. When I hold tightly to my
paintings and feel I have to sell them to live, I have trouble.
When I am doing new paintings, my old ones start to sell."
When she refocuses from the need to make money to creating new works, the older ones sell.

Attachment is a belief that you cannot create what you
want. If you are attached to having it, you fear that you
may not get it. This again goes back to a belief in scarcity,

which in turn may stem from a lack of faith in your ability to create what you want. The key issue is whether it is all right if the desired object or experience doesn't manifest.

Fear and attachment go hand in hand. You may fuel beliefs such as "I am not worthy to receive" or "Scarcity is everywhere." Focusing on scarcity attracts scarcity. However, if it doesn't matter whether it comes or not, you support the belief in abundance. You may also recognize that goals may be fulfilled in a multitude of ways. Perhaps even something better than what you asked for may come along. You need to be relaxed, confident, and trusting.

So you don't win Megabucks. Money may come in some other form. Or perhaps you attain a feeling of security and safety in your life, which was what you really wanted in the first place. You thought having a lot of money would achieve this.

Gentle Changes in Beliefs For the Slightly Skeptical

A doctor told a patient—with an advanced case of cancer of the lymph nodes—that he had exhausted all standard treatments. He begged his doctor to try an experimental drug called Krebiozen. His doctor reluctantly gave him a dose on a Friday. On Monday, the doctor was amazed to find that "the tumors had melted like snowballs on a hot stove." Within ten days the patient left the hospital cancer-free.

About two months after leaving the hospital, the patient came across some articles stating that Krebiozen had been deemed ineffective in treating his form of cancer. He suffered a relapse and was readmitted to the hospital. This time the doctor said that the drug was effective if given in the proper concentration. Of course this was not true, but the patient was excited.

The results were dramatic. The patient was once again quickly free of symptoms and left the hospital. Within about two months, the American Medical Association announced that a nationwide study found the drug worthless. This time the patient was shattered. The cancer blossomed anew and he died two days later.

Cited in many articles and books, this case is a famous example of the power of the conscious mind to heal. However, few of us are likely to respond so dramatically to external information. Many scientific "wonder discoveries" either fail or offer limited benefits and we need testing over long periods for side effects as well as favorable results.

Our scientific and medical sophistication often makes us more skeptical and this cynicism can actually work to our detriment. Since few real miracle cures occur, most physicians are reluctant to acknowledge the relationship between healing and consciousness. As patients, we are too urbane to be tricked the way this patient was. Can we bypass beliefs about our limited self-healing power? We believe so.

Let's return for a moment to Paul, the man with the painful tennis elbow. His profession required him to work continually with "objective" scientific principles and to view the body as just another machine. When his body was uncomfortable, he sought external substances (medication) or intrusive action (surgery) to restore his health. He felt he could not discount fifty years of indoctrination overnight, so he looked for a less dramatic and gentler way of dealing with his beliefs.

> The pain around the elbow was most pronounced when I played tennis and for years I tried a variety of remedies to reduce the discomfort. For example, I used a two-handed backhand, which felt awkward but did not produce as much dis-

comfort as my preferred one-armed backhand. I also wore an arm brace. However, the only real cure was many days of rest between matches. During actual play, I learned to endure pain.

A sports medicine specialist gave me some limited advice about exercising and ice packs and recommended a medication I had not tried before. Given my belief in the power of medication and the newness of the drug, I assumed I had found a wonder drug. Within a few hours I felt noticeable relief, yet it was supposed to take at least several days to have much effect.

For some reason, I knew I had found my own magic bullet. I invested tremendous power in the drug. I visualized it encircling my elbow with healing white energy.

I cut the doses in half and even took imaginary doses sometimes. I pretended to take the pill while doing a healing visualization. I had no regular pattern and followed an intuitive route as far as using it and ice packs. It didn't seem to matter what I did because the condition steadily improved.

Although I experience mild stiffness or soreness, this is extremely minor compared to thinking I might have to give up playing altogether. In any case, a residual part of myself probably is still a bit skeptical, and perhaps this is reflected in the slight, lingering discomfort.

We mention this case for those who may find it difficult to make dramatic changes in beliefs, such as the Krebiozan case. The real question is: Can you **suspend your disbeliefs** long enough to experiment with them?

Developing a belief in self-healing does not usually mean new learning as much as it involves unlearning. You must temporarily set aside the "negative" conditioning that claims these abilities are not "real."

> Since I loved taking a pill, why not enhance it so that half the medication had twice the power? Or perhaps an ice pack alone would do the trick if I had not played but just coached my son, even though coaching is just as strenuous.

Beliefs can be temporarily put on a shelf to make room for a new opening. A negative assumption can recede while a new one emerges.

> I took half the medication and visualized a full-strength effect, thus allowing my old belief to survive while I powered up the new belief. I didn't give up my belief in medication. In fact, in the beginning I actually enhanced it. But over time I put my energy in a different place, in my own capacity to heal myself.
>
> I was the experiment and the experimenter, and enjoyed the challenge of playing with my own beliefs. I did not deny them but loosened them from their hold. In so doing, they had less and less control over me.
>
> I was increasingly able to pinpoint which beliefs I gave energy to while still acknowledging the presence of old beliefs. I gradually dislodged old habits and replaced them with new beliefs. I then had choices. I could still take the medications, but I was no longer dependent on them.

For one person, her rational part made it extremely difficult to trust either her own inner power or the wisdom of the Universe. However, prayer is a form of manifesting and a familiar and comfortable form for someone who may have been exposed to it through her upbringing, as the following student was.

> Belief is perhaps the greatest obstacle because I found my intellectual and scientific side stepping in and saying, "Wait, you can't do that; it's impossible!" Then I found that whatever I thought about wouldn't happen.

> Capturing a strong belief in yourself allows a full manifestation. However, some people have trouble adopting an open belief system. I always had a hard time trusting myself. When I doubt myself, I am not able to manifest. This is why I find it easier to let manifestations take the form of prayer because it then takes the pressure off me.

> I prayed for a beautiful apartment, a hot new car, and that sick friends heal. They all materialized within a week.

> Last night I saw a stranger's car parked in our space. I prayed that it left before my boyfriend got home so we wouldn't have to call the tow truck and it was gone in 30 minutes.

> Even though I realize that prayer is a form of manifestation, I utilize this method to relieve myself of any feelings of failure if it doesn't work. Also, I find prayer meditative. Perhaps that is why the method is so effective because I let my mind and body relax so much that it takes care of what I want by itself.

Further Hints for Changing Outmoded Beliefs

Our environment powerfully shapes and reinforces beliefs. Become more aware of the environment and how it influences you. This gives you choices about how to respond or even whether you wish to create a different, more supportive environment.

What messages do you receive through interactions with your present environment? For example, do you find that your regular associates exude abundance and creativity or do they represent scarcity and victimization? Do you listen regularly to news stories about violence, lack, and fear? You can upgrade personal beliefs by avoiding people and experiences that reinforce a negative viewpoint. Instead, seek out individuals and situations that bolster positive beliefs.

Our group built upon this central premise. By exchanging support, we surpassed pre-existing limitations. For example, one member experimented with time. She drove thirty miles in such a short time that it challenged our current assumptions about time and matter. Yet she found time very fluid and encouraged us to experiment using techniques she found useful. We soon replicated her results for ourselves. The mutual support permitted us to go beyond self-imposed limitations. Another person successfully fixed her broken car radio through visualization and conscious intent, a technique that is covered in a later chapter. Again, this information gave us the courage to "repair" our own appliances.

We hadn't thought of such an experiment and were surprised with the success. Using only conscious intent, many of us found we could repair car engines, leaking pipes, and rototillers that hadn't worked for some time. Again, a supportive environment allowed us to overcome self-imposed restrictions.

Look at the larger environment, such as your neighborhood, community, and government. Do some organizations promote beliefs favoring victimization and scarcity? Do you feel the energy you spend in such groups is productive and empowering?

As previously mentioned, many of us found that watching television news—with so much emphasis on crisis, negativity, and scarcity—did not support our beliefs. Politics also reinforced helplessness in the face of large geopolitical forces and events beyond our control. The news reports crime, war, overwhelming deficits, mass starvation, and natural disasters. You may find this is not the mental environment you want either.

Explore your personal history for unresolved issues undermining your self-worth. Once you become aware, you can simply change limiting beliefs without identifying their origin. Some group members recognized their source in past family experiences. For example, one person traced the lack of belief in his own creative power to his parents' highly critical and authoritative ways.

A self-loving attitude is obviously a great asset and circumstances contributing to successful manifesting include confidence, love, and calm, centered energy.

> I am most effective when I'm relaxed, centered, in control, and have more time. Mind and emotions are synchronized with each other and I feel more love and a greater ability to visualize.

> I feel most powerful when I am relaxed, confident, happy, and connected to my heart space or inner self.

> I'm at my peak when I love myself and my esteem is high. This is also true when I am grounded emotionally, physically, and spiritu-

ally. I work with complete trust and unconditional love. Without reservation, I know all is
well. I am both in the moment and out of my
own way.

––––

When I feel balanced, open, and centered, I can
feel energy charging through my system. My
energy level is crucial for great results.

Centered energy seems to include calmness, assurance,
and confidence. An implied acceptance of oneself and others characterizes it too. Energy flows freely in such a state.
Conversely, low energy typically blocks outcomes and everything becomes a chore. Moreover, self-doubt and neediness often reduce effectiveness.

When low energy persists—and all of us spend some time
with that—it may be helpful to realize that energy ebbs and
flows. A natural balance means alternating between periods
of active and passive/receptive energy. When manifesting, you
actively put forth energy, but you must allow time for results.
Action is offset by receptiveness to the desired outcome.

In our culture, which stresses "doing" over "being," we
often resist low-energy or low-activity periods. Rather than
denying such energy, we can just acknowledge its presence
and allow it to pass through, trusting that it will shift again.
Denying its presence only infuses more sluggishness and
inhibits flow.

We must nurture ourselves in whatever way reinforces
feelings of value and self-worth. "I find that walking by a
lake during a beautiful sunset, buying a treasured piece of
music, or eating a special favorite food speeds up the energy flow," says one manifestor. We should appreciate the
abundance of what we have rather than focusing on lack.
We all have unique ways of nurturing ourselves. Find your

ways of expressing self-love and practice them. This is not a selfish act. Through greater self-love and appreciation, we more effectively support and assist others.

In addition, manifesting for others can sometimes be more effective than manifesting for ourselves, assuming the person also wants what we wish for them. Usually, when we manifest for others, fear of failure and self-worth issues are less pronounced. It can lead us to wonder what would happen if we all manifested each other's needs and desires instead of our own.

> My roommate liked a guy named Jake and really wanted him to come to a party. She invited him but he said he wasn't feeling well and also lived a good 30 minutes away. She wasn't too hopeful. I told her I would manifest that Jake would drop by and stay at least an hour.

> I consciously manifested this event both verbally and through visualization. Sure enough Jake showed up and stayed for about two hours. I saw him laughing and talking with my roommate.

> I learned that it's sometimes easier to manifest for other people because my ego doesn't impede their hopes and desires. In addition, their wish doesn't directly affect me, so I had no problem detaching and allowing the Universe to take over.

Conclusion

Manifestation is rarely a quick fix or cure-all for every desire. It is one among many tools to enrich your life through self-empowerment. As you try out these techniques—and perhaps experience what seems to be failure—don't blame yourself. Recognize that many beliefs standing in your way now have accumulated for years. They afford a kind of comfort and security, no matter how much you may wish to change them.

A few lucky people can kick habits overnight with a sharp act of will. You probably know some former smokers who successfully went cold turkey and others who took years to relinquish the habit. Unwanted beliefs—especially those reinforced by our culture—follow a similar process. You may need time to loosen and then replace them with healthier and more desirable beliefs. For many of us the whittling down and "fake-it-till-you-make-it" approach can be quite effective.

You can choose to bludgeon self-imposed limitations, or you can gently work to replace them with new attitudes and behaviors. Identify obsolete beliefs; be clear about their substitutes; and then experiment to find which approach is most comfortable.

Chapter 6

Manifestation As a Way of Life

After nearly a year of hard work, we asked members to reflect on how utilizing manifestation had changed their lives. Looking back to the early months, what was different then from the way they manifest now? Interestingly, they frequently cited the earliest exercises with parking spaces.

> The parking exercises were kind of a test. Now I don't even test that since it happened so often. When I go downtown, even to places where people never find a spot, I know I'll find one even closer than the last time.

> I don't do a lot of heavy-duty manifesting. When I pull into a parking lot, someone comes out and I get that spot with no problem. I don't write them down any longer. I just don't worry about it.

> A lot of experiences work out to my advantage when I don't consciously manifest something. It's almost as if the Universe realizes what I need and sends it.

These statements illustrate a process most experienced; the more they manifest, the less effort they deploy. In the beginning, they tested the limits of their beliefs and were often amazed by the results. They were deliberate, active, and conscious about the process. A person sought a parking place in a precise location at a certain time, or wanted a particular article of clothing at a specific price. They had definite details in mind.

Gradually, most participants found such effort was unnecessary and could even impede the manifestation if they did not detach from the outcome. One woman reported she was "not so goal oriented" and "more open to the outcome of what is there." Another noted that at first she stressed "specifics" or the "form" in which the manifestation came. "The more I let go of form, the more it works." And still another reported that she was "less controlling and demanding and more accepting."

Letting go of form and outcome is another way of saying they had more trust in their ability to create. A greater trust arose without full awareness of the process. As one man said: "I don't have proof. I don't need it. It is the healthiest way to operate. I just trust it is so." Another said he had a "greater conviction that the Universe is a friendly place and it works to bring about the highest and best."

> When things really look bad, I trust in good outcomes even when I can't see them. Internal battles become shorter and lighter.

In one case, an ex-husband harassed and stalked a woman. She hoped to write a story to raise the consciousness of the public and state legislators, who were debating a bill to make stalking a crime. She felt inadequate as a writer but had a strong desire to write something so that others might be protected. Through a series of "chance" events, a writer from the Associated Press wanted to report her story. Her main goal was to help others and she attracted someone who could generate publicity.

Others also found a "silver lining" in some experiences. Because they took more self-responsibility, they had less anger and used disagreeable experiences to assist others.

Another participant said he had "a greater sensitivity to improbable events" that seem to support his goals. He was more receptive to what was coming, even if the facilitating situation might not make sense at the time. He essentially "knew" that the present circumstance was part of a "plan," but he was not able to see that in advance. He trusted and "tuned in to whatever was out there."

During their year of practice, most participants grew quite confident in their ability to create. They became increasingly convinced that they created all their experiences.

> I now understand that I create my own reality and my attitude dictates whether a given event is negative or positive. Energy attracts similar energy. Therefore when I transmit positive energy, I receive positive energy.

> I experienced many instances of thinking or wishing for something and then experiencing a lead or some other direct event or conversation that produced the very thing I wanted. It's clear that energy does create our experiences.

> By recording manifestations I become the observer and can reflect on them, I'm also more convinced and more appreciative. Otherwise I just might chalk it up to luck or happenstance and let it be. The examination of this process is wonderful.

After awhile, writing was not necessary to convince most participants of their own power. However a few recorded everything for many months. The log itself showcased data for skeptics who needed a tangible reminder to validate this course of action.

Although manifesting parking places no longer required much effort or even interest, it still invoked unmistakable joy and fascination.

> Life flows more smoothly. Large and small goals unfold with less stress and effort. I feel like I don't have to put boundaries on my goals. Working on goals is more fun and makes life more interesting. I also feel more connected to the Universe.

> I listen more to my heart now and not my ego. I understand more about who I am. I don't have any big revelations. The many small ones make the difference. I let love and light shine through to the harried sales clerk and transform her day as well as mine. I emit energy and it comes back. My life is deeper, richer, and more spontaneous with more serendipity than ever and with a lot less effort.

> I'm also more aware of the incidents that have been a part of manifesting, whereas before I might have just called it fate. It has become a more amazing world!

> I still do parking spaces. I delight in "chance" meetings with those I needed to contact or people who profoundly affect the way I view myself and the world. I know I've drawn these people to me, as well as the larger manifestations such as education, new work, and a home. I have been successful.

The participants viewed experiences in a new light. Life became richer and more resonant. Events previously dismissed as chance took on new significance. An unplanned, accidental meeting was actually an encounter they attracted. They made connections between events even before fully comprehending their significance.

They weren't just astounded by major experiences, such as a new job or home. As one said, it is the myriad of "all the small ones that made the difference." The perceived meaning behind many ordinary experiences gives our existence a mystical quality. In the next section, we look at some examples of this ordinary magic.

Notions of Manifesting

The word notion captures the effortless way manifestors kept discovering meaning. Notion can imply a "vague thought, an inclination," or a "whim," according to Webster's dictionary. Sometimes we were surprised by the results because our intentions matched such fleeting thoughts that we were unaware of them. We then had to work back from the manifestation itself to discover its source. Retroactive analysis helped us recognize some subtle ways in which thoughts migrate to the physical world.

Of course, we may be unaware that we injected energy into a given manifestation. Yet, over time, we realized we had energized a belief. In turn, this eventually crystallized into physical form.

As autumn approached, one participant remembered that in past years it was the time when his allergies acted up. He noticed others blowing their noses and talking about allergies. Weather reports gave daily pollen counts and allergy remedies were frequently advertised in the media. He found plenty of reinforcement for the belief that "it was that time of year" when allergy sufferers give themselves permission to feel miserable. Not surprisingly, this belief supported years of his allergic suffering.

In the following manifestation, the person was barely aware that he was manifesting. However, it illustrates how we become more conscious of thoughts and desires. As this story shows, it may not always materialize in a very pleasant form.

> Recently I had nagging thoughts way in the back of my mind, such as I-need-a-vacation, I-don't-want-to-have-this-appointment, and I-don't-want-to-be-here. Well this past week a head cold answered my prayers. I spent three days in bed. As it turned out, I-don't-want-to-be-here wasn't really dominant; it was almost sub-conscious. But then again, that may very well be what made it so powerful. Be careful what you ask for because you just might get it!

But most participants recorded experiences that were overwhelmingly positive. Many of these events were minor, such as:

> Some time ago I petitioned for a greater understanding of WordPerfect's graphics and styles. I wanted to take a workshop but not have to pay for it because I simply couldn't afford it. I put that out in a fleeting request, nothing major. I just visualized the information I needed.

> Last week a friend told me he had written a course on Desktop Publishing with WordPerfect and was going to teach a free dry run. Would I be interested? It was a full-day workshop and I learned a lot about graphics and styles, just what I wanted to know!

I needed $150 for a pair of glasses. Just then a friend asked me to type up his Master's thesis for $150 and paid me in advance. It was a veritable miracle and came just when I needed it, but it wasn't anything I visualized or consciously manifested. I just knew it would be there and I didn't worry about it. Too much else was going on at the time.

I was running short of cash and needed some work. I remember praying a little concentrated wish that work came before I did anything or went anywhere. An editing request came in the mail that day. It was only a couple of hours' worth of work, but I'd say it was pretty darn fast. It couldn't have been handier. It came right to my door and I didn't even have to make a phone call.

I am a stockbroker. If you have been paying attention to the news lately, the stock market hasn't been too kind to us. My commission check is not just skinny this week; it's non-existent. So, I figured, I better manifest money from somewhere. I started meditating and thanked God for my abundance and prosperity in general. I also thanked God for sending an additional $1,500, which I needed by a certain date. I felt a warm, peaceful feeling and took that to mean I would receive it.

I then relaxed and went with the flow, knowing that my request would be granted. I also put it out of my mind. I didn't think about it or meditate again. Out of the blue, I got more than I needed. First, my wife received an expense reimbursement for $700. Then she helped a client

close a difficult transaction for another $950. My
brokerage house paid me an additional $1,000,
which I didn't know I was owed. A couple of mis-
cellaneous checks brought the total to over
$2,600.

These money manifestations were quite effortless, without great ego investment. The manifestors "put it out" to
the Universe; went on with their daily lives; and trusted
that some unseen force worked on their behalf. It was a
"little concentrated wish," a "fleeting request," or something
that they "knew" would occur. For the most part, they were
relatively detached and unconcerned about the "when" and
the "how."

It also should be noted in the last story that the stockbroker received the total income from several sources including his spouse. He was grateful for whatever income
he received, and then trusted that the Universe would bring
the income in whatever forms it wanted.

Here are some more examples that show how often solutions come quite easily if we are alert and receptive.

Today I manifested a green magic marker. On
Friday I used red and yellow ones. I wanted a
green one for a certain task. I thought that they
probably don't have green in the office and didn't
even bother to ask. At noon a coworker sat at
my desk. When he returned to his own office, he
took everything with him except a green magic
marker.

———

Several times I thought wouldn't it be nice to
have a little radio in the kitchen. I really should
buy one because the stereo is too far away. Then
a few weeks ago my fiancée showed up and said,

"Oh, by the way, I bought you this little radio."
I never thought about manifesting and didn't
make that connection until now. Maybe we work
too hard at simple things.

———

I was tossing out catalogues when I saw a cot-
ton violet dress that I've been admiring for two
years in the Spiegel catalogue. It was $68 and I
didn't want to pay that. I thought wouldn't it be
great if I could get it for $25? Then I thought:
Spiegel never reduces prices that much. Today
a Spiegel sale catalogue came and the dress was
on sale for $24.90.

———

During a meeting a man accidentally stepped
on my foot. He said, "I'm sorry, and for stepping
on your foot I'll give you these," and he dropped
nail clippers into my lap. Just that morning my
mother asked me for nail clippers. I didn't have
any but thought to myself that we do need clippers. It was just a passing thought. I could
hardly believe it when they landed in my lap.

———

After I left a job I continued to get calls at the
old number and my business partner relayed
messages. Wouldn't it be nice if I could get my
old telephone number? I thought about this for
a month. Today my ex-partner said he was moving and asked if I wanted the business number
back.

———

Before I moved here, I wanted to organize an
art show for childhood sexual abuse survivors. I
put that out to the Universe. I thought about it

and kept my mind open. Two weeks ago I saw an ad: "Wanted: Volunteers to help organize an art show of survivor art." I couldn't believe it. I called right away and met a wonderful person who is also a recent arrival.

As time approached to go back to work, I asked the Universe what I should do about my car as it shifts like a tank and I knew it would kill my painful arm. I no sooner put the thought out when my daughter called to offer her easy-driving car and we swapped cars permanently.

I saw long lines at all the supermarket checkouts. It looked like fifteen minutes minimum. I said, "I manifest a new register opening up and I'm first in line." I grabbed a newspaper to bide my time. I had just opened the paper when a clerk said, "I am making a new line and you can come over if you like."

The person in the last manifestation was quite detached and even started reading. He added that usually when a new line opens everyone rushes over. In this case the cashier walked to the end of one of several long lines and picked him out.

So many of these "ordinary" manifestations were quite effortless, accompanied by an intent or a mild desire: "Wouldn't it be nice if . . ." In some cases—such as with the green magic marker—the woman logically concluded that the office didn't have any. Yet the desire was registered and perhaps her logical deduction released and detached the desire.

Events such as these occur regularly but go unnoticed or are passed off as coincidence. By becoming more aware and appreciative, you energize occurrences and thus encourage further "little magical miracles." Begin to expect them to appear. You will enjoy a richer, more exciting, and empowered life.

Living in the Flow

During the summer, Todd and I met at his country home to work on this book. We live about thirty minutes' driving time apart. The peaceful and bucolic setting meant that we could be very productive.

We wanted to be flexible about meeting to allow for other events. After all, it was summer. Rather than fix regular meetings, we decided to intuitively connect with one another when we felt it was appropriate. As a result, the times of writing and discussion seemed to follow a natural unfolding. We found that when we called each other to discuss the book or decide on a meeting time, one's schedule almost always "fit" with the other. Usually, when one was occupied with family or other matters, the other was also busy. Our lives and the book project seemed to have a similar energy flow.

We tuned into this phenomenon and accepted where we were in it without becoming frustrated if our expectations were not met. At times chapters seemed to move very quickly; at other times we were unable to produce any material for several weeks. Although we were somewhat frustrated when things slowed down, we recognized the natural ebb and flow. We accepted wherever we were without judging the process or ourselves. We enjoyed an intuitive satisfaction and peace when we flowed naturally.

I found that even my arrival time always seemed perfect when we both trusted the flow of events. At times I would arrive considerably later than promised. This usually coincided with some task that took Todd longer to complete than anticipated. On one occasion I arrived early. I was feeling stressed and out of balance, but the time I spent alone actually facilitated our work when he finally joined me.

Each of us is a river of energy, which in turn flows as part of a larger body of water in a general direction. Our work together on the book represented streams of energy intertwined with the broader energy currents of our lives. We could flow with those energies or force a particular pace or direction. It seemed much more comfortable when we could let go and flow with the larger body of water.

This was not always an easy "letting go," since both of us were used to a certain level of organization and structure. Meeting goals and deadlines reassured us of our productivity.

The process is subtle and requires trust and a tuning inward to detect intuitive directions. You can use outward events to monitor whether you are in the main flow or rowing upstream. When moving against the current, you may feel out of balance and events do not happen effortlessly and easily. Life may seem difficult and full of obstacles. Several participants recognized this.

> When I'm calm and follow my intuition things happen just right. When I think everything through, I get out of touch. I can tell the difference and get back into the flow. Our little voices plant ideas. Wouldn't it be fun to do this or that? We need to listen because that leads us to what we want.

> I don't feel rushed or in a panic to find a job like I did last year. I feel it will come and trust my own gut instincts. When the career counseling

class was filled, I realized I so often rely on other people's opinions. If I had attended that class, I would have again asked the instructor and students to help me decide. This way I am forced to be more in tune and open to what the Universe brings. The other evening I felt fairly receptive to life and another job popped out of the paper that evening!

I find myself trying less and flowing more. I feel less in control but I am okay about it. I trust more than I used to. "Inner knowing" can be a tremendous asset. You don't have to convince anyone. It just is.

"Tuning in" is an alien concept for many of us. In the second example, we have a person who seeks external criteria for a job instead of looking within for guidance. Rather than feeling frustrated that she did not get into a class she hoped would give answers, she instead saw an opportunity to seek her own solutions, which seemed consistent with her energy flow. She could have become upset and perhaps tried to force her way into the class. In addition, enough discouragement would have led to simply giving up. She could either resist the natural unfolding or go with it and ask herself how to benefit from the experience.

When our manifestors first observed their creations and experimented by following the "little voice," "gut instinct," or "inner knowing," their lives seemed to flow more smoothly.

I needed to lighten my class load and drop chemistry but I knew my advisor would not understand since I had been out of school for almost 20 years. I thought his counseling might make it easier. Instead, I was notified that my advisors had changed.

My new counselor—a very compassionate woman—gave me support and guidance. I took a replacement course that allowed me to talk out a lot of stress. I switched from a day to an evening course in another case. Somehow I knew it was perfect that I started out in the day course as it prepared me for the evening course.

While I was switching courses, times, and advisors, a gut part of me said, "Do this or that." Following this intuitive feeling led to an incredible validation of the process.

I need some surgery now. My intuition says it is okay. I trust my relationship with my higher power.

Here a student faced many decisions. She felt uncomfortable in some classes and with certain people. She had to "intuit" her way in a relatively new environment. While listening to this inner part, she also tested its validity, making it increasingly easier to both recognize and follow its guidance. She created harmony and flow with the larger energy current, which in turn, guided and prepared her for a new career.

This last example on flow shows how little effort is required. This man only needed a clear intention and to listen to his intuition.

Each year in the fall, a nearby church has a chicken pie supper as a fundraiser. This tradition has been going on for almost 100 years. The tickets go on sale about a month before and usually sell out in a couple of days. Because it is so popular and the only advertising is by word of mouth, I have my computer remind me about six weeks ahead.

This year, when the computer message appeared, I noted my intention to attend. However, unlike past years I didn't put it on my TO DO list and forgot about it altogether.

I was hiking two days before the dinner. My intuition said to take the back roads. This route takes me past the store that sells the tickets. As I approached, I thought I should stop to see if they had any. Again my intuition interrupted and said to go on the way back, which I did without giving it another thought.

As I look back, I was surprised that my logic did not kick in with its usual advice, like, " It's too late, they are sold out." or "If they should have any tickets then stop now and not on the way back; someone else might get the last ones."

It was late afternoon when the clerk patiently told me they sold out three weeks earlier. The owner then announced that someone had just returned some tickets about an hour ago. I asked for four, as we usually ask another couple to go along. She only had two, which I took. I then gave her my name in case two more came in.

Late Saturday morning, the clerk called with two more tickets. We called the people who usually go with us, but they were busy. Then my intuition said, "Call Barry and Terri." They were delighted because they had always wanted to go.

That night as we finished dinner, Terri said that this dinner was perfect because just that morn-

ing she was dreaming of a turkey or chicken
dinner with mashed potatoes, squash and home-
made pie. She didn't want to cook all that food,
but now it had been served to her and she didn't
even have to clean up. It all just seemed to flow.

Another example might involve a canoe going down rap-
ids. The occupant chooses the destination, but the means
to that end are open and flexible. To move quickly and effortlessly, the current guides the canoe around rocks and
turbulence.

In a similar fashion you can affirm a desire, such as two
tickets to a dinner. You then trust and detach from the
outcome. After the choice is made, you gently follow a river
of life events, always aware of that inner voice, the intuitive messenger that alerts you to stop at a store even though
logic tells you it is a waste of time.

Connectedness

How often have you thought of a friend and then a few
minutes later, they call or you run into them? How does
this happen? Is this simply a chance occurrence? Does a
telepathic network connect us all? Is the bond comparable
to that of a parent and child or spouses, when each seems
to sense when the other needs assistance even though they
are physically separated?

For the participants, such coincidences were frequent. Unfortunately, we have no record of times when manifestors
thought of someone and did not link up. That situation would
have been more ordinary and would not be cause for comment. Perhaps the awareness or expectation itself might
hinder the connection. Or perhaps we do hook up but are
unconscious of the connection. Certain conditions related to
detachment and focus may precede such occurrences. In so

many incidents, the experiences themselves convinced these participants that coincidence was not operating.

Here are some of these happenstances. Are they manifestations? Please judge for yourself.

I was trying to contact a work acquaintance I don't often talk to. Her line was busy the first time. The second time, she was at that instant calling me. Instead of a dial tone, there she was and she never calls me. It was freaky that before I heard a ring, I picked up the receiver to dial her number.

———

I was thinking a lot about a friend who relocated to California because today was her birthday and we hadn't talked for a long time. I haven't even thought about her much until today. A few minutes after I got home, the phone rang and it was my friend.

———

Yesterday I thought of a friend I hadn't seen or spoken to in four or five months. They moved out of the country and for some reason stopped talking to me. At 7 A.M. she called and wanted to resume our friendship.

———

All day long, I had this nagging feeling I should call a cousin I hadn't talked with for quite a few months. When I finally called, I found out she had a bad day and was so happy I called. She was feeling devastated and depressed. It was an incredible conversation, the best we ever had. We shared a lot of great stuff. The Universe works in amazing ways.

———

I decided I would go see a business that has not advertised with us in three years. I was thinking about them a lot lately. On my way there, I stopped by the office and found a phone message from them. They wanted to get an ad in the guide. Would I come see them right away? I love it when things connect!

———

I was thinking about Fred in Austria and hoping he was having a great time. I thought it would be nice to get a post card. When I went to the mailbox at noon, there was a post card from Fred. I was really excited and realized I had a premonition.

———

I wanted to celebrate my parents' anniversary as a family. I thought wouldn't it be nice if my brother would fly up so we all could be together. It seemed unlikely, given his family situation. Today my brother called and said, "What if I come to visit?" I couldn't believe it. We call each other about once every two to three years. He had a free airline coupon that was going to waste, so it worked out great!

———

I got a message from a guy interested in buying my woodstove. I called and left another message. He called again and left a number to call that was just one digit off from his first phone number. I called, but it was obviously the wrong number. I explained the situation to the wrong-number person. Turns out, he and his wife were just talking about buying a woodstove that minute. I said, "I have an *All-Nighter*." And he said that was exactly what they wanted.

How do these manifestations fit into our previous discussions? They are so casual, that in some cases they don't even ask for a response. We may be thinking of someone but not necessarily asking them to contact us. Perhaps a wistful desire is all that's needed for a physical connection. The brother's visit unfolded even though the sister thought it logically unlikely. Once again we see the limitations that logic imposes.

As evidence that an unseen network of energy connects us all, consider the person who had a "nagging feeling" to call her cousin. Empathic ties linked the family members despite physical distance. Some kind of extraordinary communication also connected the woodstove buyer and seller. Remember those who desired certain products and "just happened" to be in a store at the right time when the item was available at an attractive price?

> I needed someone to help make wreaths for my big November show. I ran into a neighbor at a barbecue who had taken my wreath-making class and asked if I needed help. I later ran into a second woman who said she was interested too.

> I worked three jobs in the past few weeks. Today I had a time conflict with two of them, but had no way of reaching one boss to resolve the problem. For some strange reason he walked by another place I was working. He just wanted to say "Hello," so I resolved the conflict right then. The funny thing was that my boss has never just walked by to say hello. Everything worked out perfectly.

I had to get in touch with my music teacher before the evening's recital. After I missed her on the phone that morning, I realized it would be difficult to reach her. While having lunch downtown, I "ran into her" and got the information.

A friend asked me if it would be possible to use the piano in the cathedral. I offered to speak to the rector, but found out he had relocated to another parish. A short time later at the YMCA, I swam alongside the new rector and both of us got out of the water at the same time. We introduced ourselves and I asked about the piano and he said yes.

I had to contact this woman about a group boat trip the next day. I couldn't reach her by phone. While picking up some concert tickets, I just happened to run into her. The chances of this happening were very slim; a variation of a few seconds would have made the difference.

I walked along the beach picking up seashells. I came across a sand dollar with a chip. I said to myself, "I want a whole sand dollar." Within ten minutes a woman came along and handed me a whole sand dollar and told me this is very rare. Those were the only two sand dollars I saw during the four days I was there.

A friend was in an important race and asked me to send him energy. When I was in the library, I forgot about it. At about 11:30 I got this intense feeling he was having a difficult time.

So I focused on his running and sent energy to him. Next time we talked, he told me of hitting a "wall" and felt extremely distraught and just thought there was no way he could finish. He said that right around 11:30 or 11:40, he got a sudden energy spurt and continued the race.

At another time I did the same thing without telling him if or when I was sending the energy. He told me he got an energy surge right about the same time I remembered sending it. This second time was more of an experiment to confirm the first incident.

———

At a restaurant, I met a trucker who had just blown some tires. He mentioned that he never stops here and asked me what I did. I told him of my involvement in a new healing process. He said his wife had various ailments and was very interested in alternative medicine. Although quite skeptical himself, he began talking about coming to see me with his wife. The Universe evidently adjusts schedules so that meetings can come about. His tire problem made him pull off precisely where I was.

The first several incidents all relate to how we draw the appropriate people to us when we need to contact them. We also attract people when ordinary means of communication, such as the telephone, do not seem to work. The way they unfold can't be controlled or planned. This is a challenging way to learn to trust and detach from a specific plan. How could a person anticipate meeting the boss at another job, the rector at the pool, the contact at the box office, or the music teacher while having lunch downtown?

One group member was interested in connectedness and did a little experiment. As an employee at a ski resort, he was due to relieve a coworker. Since he was running late, he sent a telepathic message to another employee—who was also a friend—to do it for him. When he arrived, he found his friend had indeed relieved the regular guy, just as he projected. On the way home later, he telepathically asked his friend to stop at a particular store and buy him a drink, which he also did.

For our final set of examples we look at three cases of "connections" with nonhumans. Unlike the previous more common incidents, we only have these examples.

> For years, pigeons ran rampant and destroyed our garden. I "connected" with the birds and asked them to please go someplace else. Four weeks later the pigeons vanished. You can't imagine what this means to me, since every time I looked out the window there they were looking at me all that time. Did I really do this? I have no choice but to think I did, as I can find no other explanation. Pigeons don't just up and leave when they've nested and roosted somewhere for years.

> Our blind, deaf, and severely arthritic Shetland pony needed to be put out of her misery. I put this off but communicated with Lady that it would soon be her time. On Saturday when I fed her, I said with my mind, "Lady, if you would only die by yourself I wouldn't have to kill you but on Monday I'll have to make plans. It would be so nice if you died naturally."

> I heard about a coming snowstorm and wanted to do it before. I said to Lady, "If only you would

die this morning." When I came home for lunch my daughter said that when she went to feed Lady she found her dead and still warm. She showed no signs of struggle and was very peaceful. Yes, I do believe we communicated.

———

Dad asked my husband Dean and me to go ice fishing in his little popup shack. We didn't get any bites for almost a half hour. Finally, I said, "Look guys we have to start visualizing." His father kind of snorted and said, "Oh you think so?"

Dean and I visualized little fishies jumping onto the hooks. I just sent them love and asked them to be my dinner. Well, I swear it wasn't more than 10 minutes when the fish started biting! I got so many bites; it was hilarious.

We ended up with 15 fish over the next half hour; I caught the most, with Dean a close second. Dad had only one big enough to keep! I restrained my gloating as best I could.

No doubt many readers believe they communicate with their pets. But has a given communiqué ever been confirmed as received and understood? The first two examples are rare in our study, although other studies verify such exchanges with dolphins and plants. In these cases, the method was some form of telepathy.

The third example suggests a kind of connectedness with animals we consume as food. This manifestation would probably not sound so strange to Native Americans who usually have a more intimate and respectful attitude toward nature than most of us experience. Perhaps it was the appreciation and love toward the fish that drew them to her.

We close with an unusual example of communication that may have taken place between a human and so-called in-animate object.

> I was sitting on my porch with a friend. It was a beautiful, sunny, and cool day with a strong wind blowing. We were both tucked into our down-filled wicker chairs with light blankets, enjoying the day.
>
> I noticed an empty five-gallon pail blowing down my driveway toward the street. My driveway runs past the porch back to the barn, where I had left the bucket. I was so comfortable that I didn't want to get up to retrieve it. So I quickly visualized the bucket coming to me.
>
> At that very moment the wind stopped and the bucket was just ten feet away in the middle of the driveway. Then the most amazing thing happened. The wind shifted direction by 90 degrees and blew the bucket right to my chair. I didn't even have to move to pick it up! Then the wind changed back to its previous direction and stayed that way for the rest of the day. I know because I watched it very closely.

Conclusion

We began with everyday occurrences that we could overlook and pass off as chance and ended with some rare examples. Some type of consciousness may connect all humans and perhaps humans and other living and non-living entities. In Rupert Sheldrake's book, *Dogs That Know When Their Owners are Coming Home*, he demonstrates how certain dogs connect with their owner's minds. They seemed to know the exact time their owner decides to come home, even when separated by many miles and when the owner varies the time of arrival.

At this point we simply encourage you to consider these examples and look for them in your own life. Experiment and stretch your own beliefs to see what is possible. Look for those "chance" meetings, phone conversations, pet connections, and logically doubtful yet meaningful connections between events. Look for those events today and you will see more of them tomorrow.

The large and very conscious manifestations—such as the healed elbow or ideal job—are wonderfully challenging and significant. But our participants showed that we could live day to day in a world bordering on magic. You have only to expand your consciousness, imagine possibilities, and allow for meaningful coincidences to unfold before your eyes. Or play with your life, as the person did when the wind blew a bucket to his side.

Keep your belief in chance and fate, if you like. However, for a few moments each day contemplate that some greater benevolent power—of which you are the guiding master—can enrich your life and give it greater purpose. Try not to take this or yourself too seriously. Let it be fun! Experiment and create your own connections. Become your own teacher. No one is better qualified to challenge and teach you about these phenomena than you are.

CHAPTER 7

Are Limits Imposed on What We Can Manifest?

Alice laughed. "There's no use trying," she said. "One can't believe impossible things."

"I dare say you haven't had much practice," said the Queen. "When I was your age, I always did it for half an hour a day. Why sometimes I've believed as many as six impossible things before breakfast."

Lewis Carroll, *Alice in Wonderland*

Most participants materialized parking spaces, objects, and a wide variety of experiences. Many also increased awareness of how flow contributes to greater harmony. A few even manifested extraordinary experiences. Their accounts fired our enthusiasm to try bigger challenges. If one could do it, perhaps others could too. Of course this support was an essential function of the group. Similarly, recounting these incidents is the primary purpose of this book. This is our message: We can do it and so can you. If you are skeptical, don't just take our word for it; experience it yourself. Expand your own belief system. Ultimately, we ask whether manifesting imposes any limits.

Self-Healing

"Thy faith hath made thee whole."
(Matthew: 9:22)

Have you ever tried to console someone with a cold and have him say, "It's okay; I get a bad cold this time every year." Evidently, he not only accepts the cold, but also expected it! This example is not that different from the person in Chapter 1 who expected rain on his vacation. This is the energy he gives to the belief, which in turn attracts bad weather or illness.

One participant reflecting on health reaffirms once again how we attract what we believe:

> I frequently see myself creating illnesses while feeling helpless to alter their course. When my sons come down with the flu, I just assume I will catch it sooner or later. In turn, they often get it from classmates and it's the same illness spreading throughout my classes and in my colleagues' office buildings. At certain times of the year a sickness mentality permeates the community and becomes a hot topic. You can feel like an outsider if you haven't had an illness.

One inspired participant resisted this fatalistic attitude. Her self-healing experiences were most helpful during the Christmas season, when she had several performances planned. Neither her family nor work environment supported good health at the time, and yet she created optimum health anyway. She spent three weeks in close proximity to people with colds, including her husband. She committed herself not to succumb because of the upcoming concerts.

She described her method when she kissed afflicted family members or felt a possible symptom: She said, "I will not get this cold because I love my life—which is full of wonderful activities—and my beautiful immune system wards off this virus."

Closer to Christmas and even more performances, she detected some symptoms. Determined to be healthy for Christmas Eve, she focused energy in this direction. This presented an interesting consequence after Christmas Eve passed.

> Everyone at work had laryngitis with strep throat. I don't want it, as I am singing at two services on Christmas Eve. I decided to bolster my immune system again. So first thing every day I told my body how wonderful it is and how I can't wait to get up and begin the day. In short, I transmitted love vibrations to my immune system.
>
> I felt wonderful for both performances, but on Christmas day I felt terrible. I had a headache and sore throat that would not quit. On the night of the 25th, I realized what I had done. I had to demanifest my own script. I began movements to reverse the situation. On the 26th, I still felt bad but better so I went to work. On the 27th I felt perfectly well. All my coworkers took time off and sought antibiotics. For the second time this year, I prevented illness with my mind.

At the University of California at San Diego, sociologists found that mortality drops by 35 percent the week before the Harvest Moon Festival, an important Chinese event and a time of special reverence for the elderly. The rate rises by an equal amount the week after the festival. This suggests that people can postpone death to experience a favored occasion. The issue our manifestor faced was what to do after the concert passed. She had to recharge her immune system. Though she was already ill, she experienced rapid healing compared with her colleagues who had the same illness.

Several weeks later, she did manifest an illness at the outbreak of the Gulf War. At that time she felt helpless to do anything about it. The events were too overwhelming.

> I was depressed all day long the day before and kept saying to myself, "I am sick at heart." By afternoon I had transferred that to my body, as I felt sicker and sicker. I had to take the next day off. This was my first illness in many a moon. I enjoyed health through boosting my immune system all year, and today I manifested illness. Apparently I had internalized a perceived illness in the world.

Four days later she was still very sick. Before that, her friends, colleagues, and family members were sick, but she remained healthy. This time something more distant—the flow of world events—weakened her commitment and undoubtedly her immune system. Affirming verbally that she was sick gave the malady a physical platform. As she said several days later, "This has been a real bout, as it has been with the world."

Overcoming internalized beliefs and expectations is part of the challenge. When external authorities reinforce predispositions, our self-healing goal can be even more difficult to actualize. Let's return once again to the manifestor with the sore tennis elbow. He recalls how his family physician first prescribed rest for at least six weeks, to be followed by only periodic play.

> This was very frustrating because I wanted to play more regularly. He told me about cortisone shots, but they would also only be temporary.

> After going to a sports medicine doctor, I felt I
> had done as much as could be done medically.
> His suggestions involved painkillers, elbow
> braces, ice packs, and exercises. I was led to be-
> lieve it was a chronic condition that could be
> "managed" with proper treatment and rest. No
> one suggested that I might uproot some mental
> cause and eventually cure the ailment.

At this point the patient was grateful to find a better
way to continue athletic activities, but he was also frustrated with his inability to manifest what he really
wanted—a cure for his sore elbow. No physician offered
that alternative and he knew of no one his age, who had
cured this condition. He continued to search for that solution, "knowing" that it must be possible.

Another participant had been experiencing some bone loss
around one of his molars and his dentist recommended some
re-constructive surgery to repair the area and save the tooth.

> I didn't care for this procedure and began to vi-
> sualize the bone repairing itself. On a regular
> basis I would visualize the bone filling up the
> pocket under the tooth. When I went in for my
> normal check-up six months later, the dentist
> looked in amazement at that area of my mouth
> and said there must have been a mistake. He
> checked his x-ray that showed the pocket there
> only a few months ago. You need to understand
> that according to what dentists know, bone sim-
> ply does not repair itself. Deterioration can be
> halted but bone tissue can not regenerate. The
> dentist told me that there had to be a mistake
> with the first x-ray. He could not believe in self
> healing.

To finish this account, the subject mentioned that he knew another dentist whom he played golf with. When the other dentist heard the story, his reaction was that he was just trying to make some extra money from the dental insurance. What we found fascinating was that the golf- playing dentist would rather impugn someone in his own profession than accept the possibility that one could heal bone loss through a kind of mind over matter technique. It demonstrated to us how strong and rigid our beliefs can be.

Another participant experienced a major head injury when she was thrown from a horse. She was given only a 30 percent chance of survival. When she rebounded, her doctors were amazed but also advised her to accept her condition and the likelihood of having a long-term disability. As an avid tennis and volleyball player, she was determined to regain her previous abilities despite the grim prognosis.

> In my mind I kept saying, "I will be playing again soon." They said I probably would not talk or walk. In the back of my mind I knew I had learned to talk, walk, and eat and could learn them again. I didn't want to go to rehab. Though very compassionate, the physical therapists were also victim oriented.
>
> Everybody told me I should be happy and grateful to be alive. All I could see was that I couldn't hit the ball the way I did before. After a full recovery, I learned we can do whatever we put our minds to doing. If we can be more open, the sky's the limit. I feel so much more now than I did before the accident that we all have tremendous mind power.

Another woman told us of her experiences following her birth during a tornado, which hit the hospital.

Right after birth, the nurse ran down a flight of
stairs with me. She accidentally dropped me and
broke my back and the doctor said I would never
walk again. My mother looked at the doctor and
said, "Oh?" I was walking before I was a year
old.

When I was seven, I had polio and the doctors
said I would never walk. My mother looked at
the doctor and said, "Oh?" Within two years I
was dancing and became a professional dancer.

My 90-year-old mother just broke her leg for the
third time. The doctor told her she would be a
vegetable. She looked at him and said, "Oh?"
Mom started walking again after four months.

We do not have to look far to see where this woman picked
up a pronounced belief in her strength/abilities and deter-
mination to live according to her own agenda. Most beliefs
are rooted in family-based systems, passed on from one
generation to the next.

Both examples involve medical personnel who based their
prognosis on experience. In addition, they tried to be compassionate by helping patients accept the condition to avoid
disappointment if the disability persisted. Yet in doing so,
they unwittingly condemn patients to their disabilities.

In the second case, we were struck by the simplicity of
the mother who never doubted the healing. Perhaps she
was too naive to credit the doctors' experience and did not
view them as unquestioned authorities. Or perhaps she simply believed that no one is omniscient.

A doctor detected two lumps in my breast. I
meditated every morning about the day being
wonderful and that I'm healthy and lump-free.
I have a chi tape showing a patient having a

sonogram. The teachers surrounding him sent chi. I plainly saw the tumor shrink and then disappear.

When I was in the waiting room, I visualized those teachers transmitting chi plus I was gathering chi myself and sending it to the lumps, seeing them disappear. After the sonogram, the tech said one lump had disappeared and the other was smaller! I'm so grateful!

This person used affirmations and drew on commercial tapes for a visual image used to heal her potential cancer. She also made use of western technology to detect disease. Multiple healing modalities can be quite effective. As we just read, traditional western medicine along with alternative approaches and manifestation techniques can combine in a potent way. Work with your beliefs about healing and curing. One technique does not have to exclude another. However, you should inform your doctor of any alternatives when he/she is also prescribing traditional medications.

Another woman was diagnosed with a high risk of cervical cancer. She was told she would probably need a hysterectomy. She was frightened because she planned to start a family. So she regularly visualized being healthy by sending white light to that area. "I saw little maids dressed in black and white who cleaned spots on my cervix." She also asked herself for a reason why she had created this condition. "I thought it had to do with holding things in, not expressing myself, and not finding out who I am. I believe physical manifestations happen because of holding things in."

Over time, some group members asked her meaningful questions with increasing ease, but this situation was unusual because of the seriousness of the illness. Moreover, this woman was not a participant; she was a member's friend. Most people would probably find it difficult to accept responsibility for such a medical condition. It is one thing to wonder how beliefs prevent us from having a sunny vacation; it is another to accept responsibility for a precancerous condition that is likely to require a hysterectomy and eliminate the possibility of bearing children. For this woman, the visualization may have worked: The condition disappeared and she later became pregnant.

We close this section with a manifestation that uses both traditional medical treatment and visualization. On the one hand, we cannot know which method was responsible for the healing. On the other hand, it did work. Many of us still feel a certain comfort with the medical model, it shows how one can take the best from two different approaches and maximize the probability of rapid healing. The manifestor herself had little doubt that the effectiveness referred to the combination of conventional and nontraditional methods. Again, this experience supports our premise that belief rather than method produces desired outcomes.

> When my car was stopped, I got rear-ended by someone going 35 to 50 miles per hour. I was in considerable pain from snapping my neck. My doctor said it was quite severe and would take several months of treatment.
>
> I studied the x-rays closely so I could understand and see the damage clearly in my mind. I then asked the doctor to show me a normal x-ray so I could compare. I then put both pictures in my mind and brought the photos home in case my visualization got fuzzy.
>
> I saw the doctor three times a week; got ultrasonic heat treatment; did exercises; and beefed

this up with a massage. I used my own treatment of powered-up visualizations. I called on
my spirit guide and his band of angels to assist.

I often visualized many angels massaging my
neck. I saw the angels put the out-of-place parts
back into position and healed all the injured
spots with this wonderful warm white light
emanating from their hands. I also did a healing tape with water and dolphins.

Any time I power up, I balance it with the same
amount of gratitude. The massage was also important, since it was just joy-type work. This
balance is critical for me—activity and rest combined.

A month later, the doctor noted how "remarkable" her
healing was. He treated several others with the same injury but they "had terrible neck and arm pain and many
were crippled up and couldn't sleep."

This last account is striking because the subject did not
hesitate to use every possible resource to create a team of
helpers: a traditional medical doctor, a masseuse who also
did healing, and even a group of visualized angels massaging her neck. "I needed a caring team who believed in healing." She took an active role in her own healing, which gave
her confidence and ultimately brought success.

Manipulating Time

In his book *Unconditional Life*, Deepak Chopra tells of a
small group of miners trapped underground after a mas-
sive cave-in. They realized that the mineshaft air would
only last a few hours. Only one miner wore a wristwatch
and lied when reporting the time: When two hours passed,
he announced it was just one hour. To the rescuers' aston-

ishment, all were found alive after six days, all except the miner with the wristwatch. He could fool the other miners, but he couldn't deceive himself.

Manifestations around time began with one member and spread like wildfire in our group. The initiator wanted more time for her personal life by getting more accomplished in a given period. She also wanted to be more punctual.

When she wanted a class she was teaching to go faster, she could condense time and the class would speed up. She could also expand time, doing housework in half the usual time. But her most spectacular feats concerned arriving at a particular time. For example, when she obeyed speed limits and hit all green traffic lights, she had a fifteen-minute route to school. Yet she found that her time extensions allowed two stops on the way and she still arrived on time.

Again and again she projected arriving somewhere at a certain time, even when it seemed impossible. "I left home at 6:00 and planned to arrive at 6:45 without speeding. I wanted all green lights. I hit two red lights, but reached the driveway at exactly 6:45." Again, we must focus on the end result and not worry about how it is accomplished.

Different methods help us manipulate time. This woman did it "by visualizing arriving at a certain time." She also visualized the time on her clock radio slowing down. "I have done this ten times this month to the same destination and achieved the same results each time."

Another participant tried this when he was late for a doctor's appointment.

> The trip normally takes 35 minutes, but I had only 23 minutes. I wanted to be there at 1:00 but thought it would be okay to be five minutes late. I couldn't quite believe I made up that much time. I focused on seeing the clock in my mind

displaying 1:05. I arrived there exactly at 1:00.
I don't know if this was a miss, since I projected
being a bit late. But I do know that I arrived at
my ideal time. Something overrode my doubts.

Based on the teacher's success, this man tried it and told
the doctor's receptionist, who in turn tried it and told her son.

At my next visit, the receptionist successfully
did the same thing. Moreover, her son also man-
aged to project his destination times.

Just as this had spread within the group, it was now
becoming popular outside as well. Here is a sample of other
members' experiences:

I left my house late. I had less than fifteen minutes to get to the cafe. I was confronted with
one red light after another. I envisioned I would
arrive at the same time as my friend and the
precise time would not be important. I walked
in just as she got there and amazingly the clock
said noon exactly.

———

I only had 20 minutes instead of the needed 30
to meet my friend. So I really pulled my car
ahead. I did not look at a clock but did see myself getting to her house at the agreed time. I
made it! I don't know whether I expanded time
or moved through space differently but something happened. It was an interesting experiment in car pulling and time expansion.

———

At 8:30 I came to a closed bridge. I was supposed
to be at school by 9:00, I turned around and
started to fly. I got caught in traffic at a very

busy intersection at 8:45. Then I thought of calming down and concentrating on an 8:57 arrival. I stopped looking at my watch. I arrived at 8:58.

———

I still condense time when I'm running late and it often works. One time in particular the Universe responded in an unusual way. I needed to be at a meeting at 11:30, and visualized arriving punctually all the way there. When I pulled into the lot, the clock said 11:38. My disappointment faded when I realized I was the first to arrive. Everyone else was late, so my arrival time was still okay.

———

I told my friend in New York I would turn into her driveway at exactly 8:00. At the rate I was going, I could not make it by then. I pictured the car's clock displaying 8:00 every hour of the trip. Sure enough, I arrived on time.

I don't know how I did it given the amount of time I had to travel. I drove a little faster but not enough to make a difference. I played with time in my mind and pictured getting there. Sure enough it happened.

———

Today my kids and I drove to Virginia. The kids asked me to manifest the arrival time. I told them 5:28. I arrived exactly at 6:00, but it occurred to me that I had told my sister-in-law that we would be there by 6:00 or I would call.

Driving back, I told the kids 5:28 again. I literally didn't look at the clock for about three hours, but when we turned into the parking lot, my son said, "Look at the clock." After I parked, it said 5:28 exactly.

Several observations are worth noting about arrival times. The first is that we sometimes get what we really need rather than what we think we want. The man who wanted to arrive at 1:00 was unsure of his ability to manifest that time because it seemed a bit beyond what he could accept. The woman who was disappointed for not being on time for the meeting was still the first to arrive, which was essentially her goal. Not being late and not keeping others waiting was more important than being on time.

Relaxing during the trip and being confident of the outcome seems helpful. A sense of lightness and detachment combined with a clear focus on the arrival time worked for many. Not looking at a clock and checking for progress were also necessary elements. Constantly verifying is an indication of doubt; energizing any misgivings produces failure to arrive at the desired time.

Belief about time can manifest very simply. One participant casually asked a banker when he got to work. Without hesitation, the banker said, "7:26." His acquaintance remarked that this was a rather odd time to begin work. "That's not the time I start work," the banker replied, "That's the time I always arrive." He added, "It doesn't seem to matter when I leave home. But I notice I **always** get here at 7:26."

The power of habit and belief is illustrated in this little example. Although not familiar with our concept, he was still practicing this principle. He simply "knew" he would always arrive at 7:26 and he did!

Mind Over Matter

Can thoughts affect matter? Before my involvement in this project, I demanifested clouds at the beach. I never picked a very large cloud because I knew my own disbeliefs would get in the way. I chose a small one and focused my attention. Then I would close my eyes and visualize the cloud becoming thinner with wisps of it sheering off and spreading in all directions. I would open my eyes and see it smaller than before and then repeat the process until it totally disappeared. I did this many times and was almost always successful. When it didn't work I recognized that my ego was involved. Perhaps I had told someone I could do it or I worried what would happen if it didn't work. Once I manifested a small cloud where I had previously demanifested one. For some reason I never tried it again.

On another occasion, I also had a feeling–nothing I could prove–that at an outdoor concert a large group held off a predicted shower until the concert's conclusion. The rain began as we returned to our cars.

One participant related a similar incident at a different concert. "It started as a mild drizzle and what went through my mind and maybe others' minds was, 'I hope it stops.' And it did! Coincidence many would say, but as soon as the concert was over, it began to come down hard, as if everyone let go of the 'Don't rain' thought together."

But could we alter mechanical things and solid objects simply by using our minds? I read about a famous study by Robert Jahn and Brenda Dunne from Princeton's engineering department. A group of volunteers in front of a random number generator influenced the number of 0s and 1s simply through desire. Also, one group member used her mind to "soften" the molecules of a spoon handle so it would bend like a piece of warm licorice.

Another manifestor used Liquid Plumber to clean a clogged bathroom sink. Unfortunately a small leak appeared in the plastic pipe, and he was about to call a plumber when he thought of visualizing a repair. After all, it was only a small leak. Another participant reports a similar story:

> My bathtub faucet dripped steadily. I tried to stop it with my intent and sent out that desire several times a week. I also visualized a substance plugging the leak. For several months it stopped for a few days and then started again. Eventually it stopped permanently, although I could not pin down the exact time this happened because I had kind of given up. Maybe it would have happened anyway. Maybe.

Even since we moved into our apartment, we had a weird problem with the TV. We had to push Power then the 3 button. Then we could change channels through the remote control. So we turned the TV on and pushed 3. The only problem was that when we sat down, the TV would switch itself to channel 2 so we only saw fuzz. Then one of us would have to put it on 3 again. We had to keep getting up and doing this over and over. Obviously this got pretty annoying.

One night my roommate and I talked about manifesting while watching TV. The TV was up to its same old tricks so we decided to manifest the problem away. We immediately forgot about it and got sucked into the program.

When the show was over we realized that the TV hadn't switched channels once. We both just looked at each other and didn't dare to say anything more than, "Do you realize what happened?" because we both knew we had fixed it. After that night we never had a TV problem again.

Earlier we told the story of the broken ejector on the car tape player and how two group members were determined to manifest a "miraculous" repair through combined visualizations. Their attachment to a fixed outcome probably slowed it down, but one day a passenger fixed it quite effortlessly. He "coincidentally" had a tool kit with him.

The car radio repair inspired the following incident. The woman drove 80 to 100 miles daily and loved the radio. She had increasing problems with it for over a year and brought it to a repair shop several times. Finally they told her she needed a new one, to the tune of $160.

> I sort of gave up on it and fantasized on what a neat thing it would be if we humans really could manifest repairs. We might not have such a solid waste problem. I thought that if I meditated on the vibrations around the radio, I could fix it. I went at it mentally with firm intent. I thought it was a lark, but why not? I'd have fun with it anyway.

> A day later, the radio came on, but then conked out. So I thought, why not try again? It happened about 15 to 20 minutes after I started meditating. I did this several more times and then it stayed on permanently. I had to believe it would work. I really believe I did this with my mind! Wow! I could put radio-repair folks out of business.

It is interesting that she was successful when she had "given up" and thought she would "have fun with it anyway." It took several meditations to create a "permanent" repair. As she remarked, "I had to believe it would work." This repair inspired another participant:

> After the meeting, I thought about my radio, which hasn't worked in over a year. I raced upstairs to my old bedroom and darned if that radio didn't come on loud and clear. I couldn't believe it, but I told my mom, who had been having trouble with her radio. She said her radio began working too.

This story is similar to the "flexible time" experiment when one person told the receptionist his experience and she in turn told her son. Breaking through limitations of former beliefs can be very exciting. Once one person does it, the possibilities open for the rest of us. We constantly learned how self-imposed limitations could be challenged and altered.

Several group members found car repairs a fruitful area for manifesting. Caught in heavy traffic, one person's engine temperature rose rapidly. "I visualized white light coming down through me to surround the car and move to other cars. The temperature dial steadily decreased to below the halfway point, where it stayed."

Another member wrote that her seat belt did not work and she "did not want to spend $200 to fix it." Though she didn't work very hard on manifesting a repair her story illustrates the importance of effortlessness and detachment.

> I said, "Wouldn't it be nice if it healed itself? If it doesn't, I'll get it fixed when I can afford it." I didn't say it very often. I didn't have much attachment to whether it worked or not. I gave it up to the Universe. Soon after I noticed the seat belt worked again.

One member was strapped for money and her car needed a mandatory inspection. She could not afford to repair the faulty engine. The mechanic warned her of a "rod that blows through the piston; goes through the engine; and then the car is finished." Obviously he couldn't sign the papers because of this. She knew little about cars but visualized the engine's interior, as best she could.

> I did it with my huge planetary healing wand and programmed the crystal in the car. Every time I get in I'm healing her. The noise went away after the first day and I haven't heard it since.

Needless to say, the mechanics were amazed when the car passed inspection. A year later the same mechanic still remembered the incident and told another group member, "We had a client who fixed her car with crystals. We told her it was hopeless. I can't explain how she did it." She sold the car soon after. A year later, the new owner says it still runs.

One group member inherited a rototiller, which worked fine at first but then the gearbox froze up. His mechanically inclined brother-in-law realized the whole gearbox would have to be replaced. Instead of paying a major repair bill, he decided to manifest a repair even though this went against his conventional beliefs. His account illustrates his own resistance to a new set of beliefs.

> At first I was reluctant to try. After all, I would feel pretty dumb if it didn't work. I mean I saw the gears and my whole life experience as an engineer said it could not be fixed without major mechanical work. I did know about group members who fixed radios this way.

> I realized I had a lot of support for my conventional beliefs, but only a few second-hand accounts about manifesting. Knowing that beliefs

affect manifesting, I faced the problem of discarding my entrenched beliefs and embracing new ones. I was sure this would take a lot of energy.

Not liking this choice, I decided not to change my beliefs. After all, they have served me well. Instead, I just put them aside and allowed an opening for other possibilities. With this in mind, I approached this as an experiment.

I started to visualize. At first I had trouble focusing energy and getting a clear image. When I paid attention to my little voice, I realized I had a problem with the timing. Fixing it instantly was too big a leap and my little voice delivered many doubting messages.

When I gave the process three weeks I was able to quiet the voice. At this point I had a clear image of myself using the tiller and it worked just fine. When I reached this point I just let go and trusted the Universe to take care of the details. I felt good and was not invested in the results. I just knew that whatever happened would be okay.

I did not give it another thought until about five weeks later when I came across my tiller. So I started it up and it worked great. I was amazed to find that I was not surprised when it worked.

Then logic kicked in: In some way I had to make sense out of all this. The only way I could do it was to classify this as a fluke. At the same time this internal dialogue was going on, another part of me observed this chatter. I noticed how hard I was trying to fit this experience into my present belief system. At the end I dropped the logic, accepted the experience as such, and gave thanks that my tiller was fixed.

Many of us are programmed to only trust a certain set of beliefs rooted in Newtonian principles about the solidity of matter. Therefore, to accept the power of mind to fix things is extremely challenging. Note that this person did not give up his beliefs. He simply put them aside temporarily and treated the situation as an experiment. He knew the boundaries and accepted where he was at the time. Thus he did not set an "unreasonable" time limit for the repair to manifest. He released it and detached from the outcome. He actually forgot about it.

Some circumstances led him to the tiller some five weeks later to discover that it worked again. Even then, he had to struggle with the desire to appease his "alternate" belief system by attributing the result to a "fluke."

Perhaps the most interesting manifestation of this nature for us (the authors) happened when we tried to videotape interviews for a television series. We taped in a private home and borrowed a studio camera and the peripheral equipment.

We had several interview subjects lined up that afternoon. Gayle was from out of town and had only a short time to share her story. Because of the difficulty of getting access to this sophisticated equipment, all interviews had to be carefully organized, so time was very precious.

To our great consternation and frustration the audio would not work no matter what we did. We repeatedly shot the same scene only to learn afterwards that the sound was defective. We didn't want to inconvenience Gayle and were afraid we would fail to record her exciting account. We were getting desperate so Fred dashed back to the studio to see if he could borrow another camera.

While Fred was gone, Jane joined us. She watched us frantically trying to fix the camera wondering whether some button or cord failed to activate. After observing our mounting frustration, she calmly asked, "Why don't you just manifest the camera working?"

Everyone stood there in stunned silence. Here we were, listening over and over to successful manifestations about fixing broken machines using only visualization. Yet, none of us thought about this obvious solution ourselves.

We all looked at each other and had the same expression on our faces. Why didn't I think of this? Then each person settled into a calm state. We all visualized the camera functioning properly and everything eventually working out. The whole process took less than a minute. No other adjustments were tried.

Of course, the camera and sound performed flawlessly the rest of the day. The manifestors showed no amazement. We expected it to work and it did. The strange part was that no one thought to do this earlier. Sometimes you can be too close to your subject.

Conclusion

Are limits imposed on what we can manifest? We have found none, except those provided by our own imaginations and the limits we accept regarding what we have been taught. We know of numerous documented cases of people walking over burning coals without injury. Though no one has walked on water, we all know of one religious figure who reportedly did so. It is undoubtedly possible to walk on water, but truly believing it requires a huge leap of faith. Nobody has actually done this, so we have no experience to consider or replicate.

Of course, limits have value. The predictable offers comfort and security and it can be frightening to tinker with what we believe is normal and possible. If you want, try working with your present beliefs. Accept that all current beliefs about limitation are fine. Such self-acceptance gives you an opening for change.

If using mental power to fix a car engine is too challenging, then repair a small leak or perhaps encourage a cassette recorder with some minor flaw to perform more efficiently. If you must believe that it fixed itself without conscious intervention, then work with that premise. Perhaps the leaky pipe just happened to have a plug of toothpaste solidify over the small hole. If your belief system requires rational understanding, then respect that. Give it some information, and try to stretch the belief a little further next time.

Be gentle with yourself. You are beginning to create an entirely new way of looking at the world around you.

Chapter 8

Transforming Our Perceptions

As the group practiced for several months, we noticed a perceptual change. We became more aware of the link between beliefs and events. We were more likely to look into our thoughts, wishes, and feelings when puzzling situations occurred. In other words, we accepted responsibility for what transpired. We also noticed a greater appreciation of the way occurrences presented themselves from moment to moment. We found that the flow of experiences had greater meaning and significance.

A broader transformation also occurred: An increasing awareness that we could view life as a series of learning opportunities. Even when we underwent hardship, we found these challenges to be opportunities for growth and happiness. As we absorbed more responsibility, we realized we were never victims. Even adversity brought further opportunities for growth, and we found ourselves achieving goals in ways we could never have anticipated.

Discovering and Changing Root Beliefs

When most of us began, we chose manageable goals, which offered immediate and verifiable feedback. This was important because of our initial skepticism, and it fortified an evolving trust in our own creative powers. The process was both conscious and concrete. A parking spot was a good starting place as it was something most of us frequently needed. It was immediately verifiable and allowed us to practice detachment. Early goals involved articles of clothing, small personal items, and convenience in daily events.

However, most of us also wanted meaningful experiences. We wondered if we could also materialize complex and challenging goals. We often reversed the process: We examined what we actually had for its underlying belief pattern. If we created everything, then we wanted to understand the origin, even for situations that at first appeared to be out of our control.

We consciously wanted more money or time, but sometimes found ourselves with less. Therefore, some subconscious belief must be sabotaging us. Like detectives, we ferreted out the obstructions. Deep down, did we believe in scarcity? Did we unwittingly nurture feelings of unworthiness, or guilt about abundance? Any of these might plug up the works.

Identifying counterproductive beliefs wasn't enough. We also had to recognize how we fed energy to them, which could create even more scarcity. As manifestors, we needed to be aware of where we place energy and then learn how to change that.

For example, suppose that a woman lost money on an investment. She could conclude that she was not good at handling money. In turn, this might confirm an original core belief in scarcity. Her response might also manifest future scarcity. She might find it increasingly difficult to escape the ever-deepening cycle and replace it with a belief in prosperity.

To make this kind of change usually requires considerable practice and perseverance because of the habit's deep-seated nature. Imaginative little tricks can help; such as pretending one has sufficient income by donating to a favorite charity. Being open to receiving abundance in whatever form it comes—rather than being attached to a particular outcome— can also prove fruitful. The lottery is only one way to attract money.

It has been said that one's attitude determines one's altitude. For example, by learning from a sour investment, this woman can open the door to lucrative opportunities. She might target financial instruments that intuitively "feel right," even if they are not completely logical, trusting that they will lead to abundance.

Our group found that by expecting success and preparing for abundance, it did materialize. When we focused on failure or played victim, we sometimes overlooked opportunities in plain sight. When one door closed, we found it helpful to look for another one opening.

We worked with deeply ingrained beliefs, especially in dealing with mechanical objects. The "machine" could be the human elbow, a car radio, or a rototiller. Our root belief dictated that only physical intervention could repair an object, yet we found many instances when mind power also worked. Each manifestor confronted core beliefs; set them aside temporarily; and then dealt with them when they re-emerged. Such beliefs refer to years of societal teaching and reinforcement. To surpass this kind of thinking took time and practice.

We described how one person successfully manifested a repaired rototiller. Several weeks later, he wondered if it would still work. Doubt crept in and he was afraid to try again. What if it didn't work? Would that make him a failure? He hesitated to try. Though he feared it would not work, he eventually approached the rototiller again. Not

too surprisingly, it did not work the second time and perfectly reflected his doubt. Years of scientific/engineering
training and experience repairing machines had fortified a
pervasive belief in "material" solutions.

We also discussed a woman who created a car repair.
Had she manifested the rototiller repair, it would have
likely been successful. She was not a scientist and wasn't
even sure what a car engine looked like, much less how
rototillers worked. For her, it might have been much like
manifesting hard-to-get concert tickets or the perfect out-
fit for a friend's wedding, a dress that also was on sale.

We also saw that we can work with traditional beliefs
rather than struggling to replace them. When we are obsessed with overriding traditional beliefs, we signal that
these beliefs can't be changed. This obsession actually infuses energy to and strengthens the old belief. The key is to
work with and release this original belief while deepening
our trust and developing replacement beliefs. The person
with the tennis elbow worked with a sports medicine doctor first; then experimented with the doctor's suggestions.

> Sometimes after playing I experience some dis-
> comfort and doubt. At such times, I don't hesi-
> tate to use a mild pain killer or anti-inflamma-
> tory. Other times I won't need any medication,
> even after playing very vigorously. I felt confi-
> dent that my body handles whatever healing is
> needed. I asked what it needed and it would tell
> me.

This combined approach was also illustrated with the
woman who injured her neck in a car accident. She used a
regular doctor along with "powered-up" visualizations and
a "band of angels." She healed rapidly. A scientist could
not be sure which method contributed, but from the subject's

point of view it was the entire healing "package" that provided success.

We suggest that you view manifestation as a powerful tool. It need not substitute for any other firm belief. You are unlikely to change a root belief or an established habit "cold turkey." Instead, you can experiment with new beliefs and use them in conjunction with traditional ones. Be clear about what you want and then be open to how your goal materializes. Do not limit the Universe to a single way.

The participants learned a valuable lesson with the malfunctioning cassette ejector. Hoping for a "miracle" repair by using mind-over-matter techniques was fine, but he limited himself and "pushed the envelope," so to speak. His beliefs were still anchored in the laws of physical matter. His passenger just happened to have a tool kit and within ten minutes fixed it, after weeks of forcing a "miracle" manifestation. He could have saved himself effort and frustration with a general manifestation of a repair and let the Universe decide how it would be carried out. As it turned out, the repair conformed to his belief system in mechanical solid objects.

Of course manifestation is just one more tool for creating desired outcomes. Experiment and learn when it's most useful. Stretch your beliefs for fun. Life does not have to be a struggle. It can be lived with less effort and more efficiency if we so choose.

Manifesting with Effortless Flow

When many of us began, we were very deliberate, specific, and conscious. We gradually became less calculated and detailed. After a year of enjoying all kinds of material objects, one woman was even getting bored.

> I didn't even think of recording the drapes as a manifestation. I want the big stuff! This is so

mundane. This is just living. These things fall
into place for us all. I want miracles. I want to
be able to change the world. I want to change
everybody and not just change the drapes to
make a nice home.

For others it was not so much a need to move on to bigger miracles. They were pleased that manifestation had
become part of their lives. As one participant said, "I don't
actively manifest very often because it's so integrated now
and not a big deal. So stuff just happens, and I forget I
manifested for them."

We discussed manifesting as being "in the flow" of life.
Our subjects saw this as "things falling into place." Events
transpired effortlessly in some perfect manner. As alert
observers, the group appreciated how beautifully events
and experiences seemed to fit together. We recognized that
we created the events, but the intent was much more subtle
than some of our initial manifestations. Sometimes we only
really remembered the intent after it had already manifested.

One manifestor wanted to change a doctor's appointment
to a different date and for a shorter time. He did nothing
except think that a different appointment was more appropriate to how he was feeling now than when he made
it four months earlier.

Within a few days the doctor's receptionist asked if he
could switch his time to a shorter session on a new date?
Needless to say, the new date was convenient. Why did
the receptionist call? Was this coincidence? He had expressed no interest in changing the time and date, so how
did she know?

A teacher had written to the mother of a teenager who
had vandalized a building, offering to help in any way she

could. Although no formal meeting was planned, she began to "coincidentally" run into her.

> Twice since then, I bumped into her at the fit-
> ness club and chatted with her about her son,
> her fears, and frustrations. The interesting part
> is that I never saw her at the gym before, even
> though we both have been members for quite
> some time! Of course we were meant to see each
> other. I even parked next to her once in an area
> of the parking lot I don't normally use. But for
> some reason I drove to it on that day.

She had a simple intent and never arranged a meeting,
yet her desire to help and the mother's likely need for counseling drew them together. Why did they not recognize each
other before this? Why did she drive to a little-used area of
the parking lot that day? She knew they "were meant to
see each other."

With time and experience we become more aware of the
effortless perfection of life unfolding. One evolved participant wrote about buying a new car.

> I thought it would be nice to get a new car at
> some point. I loved my current car but it was
> beginning to rust after six years and the repair
> bills were mounting. The clutch was going and
> another major repair bill was looming.

> My desire for a new vehicle was mostly a gentle
> intent and I was not putting much effort into
> manifesting. When I did, it passed through my
> mind that I would get the same make and model
> but perhaps it would be red instead of tan. These
> fleeting thoughts occurred when I felt the soft
> clutch. My car felt less and less comfortable and
> my desire to feel safer increased.

One sunny Friday I had no obligations whatso-
ever. Yet I did feel the day would be productive
in some way. As I opened the newspaper my eyes
were drawn to a large back-page ad for a big car
sale. Usually I overlook this page, but I kept
reading and saw the color, make, and model I
had thought about.

Nine hours later I had a brand new car fully
paid for. The salesman was perfect and led me
to what I really wanted instead of a cheap imi-
tation.

Things I hadn't seriously considered suddenly
made sense. It was more expensive and had
more options than I had originally considered,
but it was exactly what I really wanted and
was perfect for my budget. I just happened to
have enough to easily cover it. The car was
emerald green instead of red, yet I knew it was
what I wanted. It looked beautiful and felt so
comfortable. The salesman even had trouble
finding it on the lot, as if it had been put aside
for me.

Sometimes we get in the way of "flow." The following
example shows how one manifestor recognized this and
decided to "ride the horse the direction it was going."

I remember once trying to find parking at a favorite beach for my 85-year-old mother and
myself. I became increasingly frustrated as I
drove round in circles in a packed parking lot
with no luck. Just when I spotted one, some teenager cut in front of me. Finally, I admitted to
myself that my mother and I were not supposed
to be there. I let go of the anger and frustration.

> While driving home, we noticed a favorite res-
> taurant and decided to have lunch. It was very
> busy, but we were immediately seated, had a
> delicious meal, and watched some dolphins frol-
> icking below us in the harbor, a rare event. As
> we left, I noticed it was overcast, the wind had
> picked up, and it was definitely not a beach day
> after all.

Another woman noted, "I think I'm finally seeing why
things happen as they do." She planned an event for a sunny
day that turned out to be rainy.

> The rain could have been a disaster. But it led
> to some wonderful opportunities. The whole set
> of circumstances just flowed from one good situ-
> ation to another. If it hadn't rained, I never
> would have gone, and I'm sure I wouldn't have
> allowed enough time to do what we did.

As we become more familiar with manifesting, we recognize more and more that we always manifest exactly what
we need. Sometimes it is immediately apparent. Other
times it may be difficult to understand why seemingly bad
things happen to good people. Ultimately we begin to learn,
as one person put it, "Bad manifestations are actually good
ones whose value takes longer to recognize."

Manifestations as Learning Experiences

The person mentioned earlier who was being stalked by
her former husband wondered why she had attracted to
herself this fearsome experience. Because of this incident,
she had to ask herself questions about her own worthiness
and her persistent role as a caretaker in a relationship. It
also stimulated her to tell her story to a newspaper reporter
who was writing an article on this phenomena just as the

state legislature was considering a bill to make such actions a crime. "It was very satisfying knowing I might help someone. I always knew something positive would come out of this experience."

Participants increasingly saw how all events had meaning. The man with the tennis elbow was, on one level, trying to wean himself from his dependence on traditional medicine. On another level, he learned why he had created this weakness in the first place.

> A major breakthrough to a more permanent cure came while co-coaching with my partner in preparation for a challenging match the following day. We both played very hard that evening, since we would be doubles partners the following morning. After we finished, I was surprised that I experienced no elbow discomfort. However, the next day after playing three sets, I had great pain again. I played just as intensely the first time, so why didn't it hurt then too?
>
> I figured it out. In one instance I competed and in the other I empowered my partner to improve her game. I wanted her to play at her best and she wanted the same for me. It became clear that I dealt with a longstanding issue about proving self-worth through being better than someone else. As a child, I learned to excel and win from my father. Living up to his expectations was the source of much dissatisfaction throughout my life.
>
> When I changed my mode to one of coaching others, it always worked. Even when I played competitively I helped opponents improve their game, even if it meant some decrease in my own. I realized I had created this elbow problem as a

learning tool, and as I learned, the pain disappeared. When I don't emphasize winning, I play better; flow more; and enjoy the game more. My longstanding major goal was to create more joy and this experience accomplished that.

Several months later he played with his son and noticed considerable elbow discomfort that evening. Was the old problem returning? They had played very hard but he didn't feel he had been particularly competitive. Upon further reflection, he realized he focused on his son's competitiveness.

I really wanted him to improve so he would get a starting position on the school team. They won the state championship for the past four years and I was worried he was not good enough to win a starting role. I had simply transferred my competitive desires to my son.

Gail Devers, the 100-meter gold medallist in the 1992 Summer Olympics, had to overcome serious illness to compete. She was once within two days of having her feet amputated. How she perceived her handicap is truly remarkable. In an interview with a news reporter she discusses her transformation.

My mental preparation is faith in myself. I wouldn't wish Graves' disease on anyone. But I'm thankful for going through it. It changed me and made me stronger. After going through all this I thought, "There's no obstacle I can't get over." I felt like I wanted this race more than anyone.

Rather than viewing herself as a victim, Devers saw the horrible disease as a source for reinvigoration and a learning experience. She was "thankful for going through it."

About uncomfortable or frustrating experiences in her life, one woman said, "Bumps motivate me. If it gets too easy, I get lazy. So I find some way to screw up and get back on track."

> If I keep affirming when things go well, maybe I won't have to manifest the bumps to stay on track. I try to take responsibility and learn from everything. I always ask what I have to learn from this experience and why things happen that way. It is a constantly evolving process.

"Bumps," as she calls them, are her teachers and keep her in the learning mode. No experience is either good or bad. They are just created situations and she always has full freedom to choose a response. She can select the role of victim or student. She can learn and grow, or ignore opportunities for lessons and perhaps create even more dramatic bumps down the road.

> As the lessons got harder, my learning process speeded up. It has become more efficient. I'm seeing more clearly my part in things and how my behavior, thought patterns, and belief systems work.

These learning opportunities can often be part of a major long-term goal, such as a romantic relationship. One man achieved his goal by manifesting his "dream" woman. He noted how his girlfriend arrived in his life, "The way everyone said it would: when I wasn't looking." He also makes a pertinent observation about what happens after a long-awaited goal materializes. When one manifests, another desire replaces it. "With our relationship's ups and downs, I attracted the perfect woman to invoke those issues I needed to work on."

The following example concerns one woman's long-desired romantic relationship. This story illustrates how life teaches and facilitates obtaining what we really want. She previously had two major relationships. Each time, she felt hurt and disappointed, but she also learned something. Her most recent relationship with a multimillionaire was very attractive since she was barely supporting herself by domestic cleaning. Nevertheless, it turned out that he wanted a personal servant, someone to wait on him. The past came back to haunt her and demanded that she heal it. She was being asked to transform a longstanding perception. She recognized that she attracted this "test."

> The Universe wanted to give me something to stand up to. He was demanding and manipulative. In the past, I gave up everything for the sake of the relationship. I gave my all asking for love in return. That situation was a huge challenge and he was a formidable teacher. I hope I never get tested again.

> Ultimately I had to rely on myself for happiness and a sense of wholeness. Once in a while I get lonely for someone to put my arms around. Those periods are diminishing in both intensity and frequency. I don't get lost in those feelings. It will happen when it's right. I've always got myself.

> Every relationship offers an opportunity for growth. You prepare yourself for the ultimate one. You attract flawed partners to help you meet challenges. I achieved this with the last relationship. I finally understood I could be alone and earn enough to support myself. If I don't have real love, I don't want a relationship.

Over time, several relationships helped to mirror what she needed to learn. She pinpointed the flaw that helped her attract a healthy relationship. But she would not experience this until she achieved her own health. She attracted several men who treated her as a servant, reflecting her own low self-esteem. Instead of feeling discouraged, she saw each as a learning experience guiding her toward a loving and healthy relationship.

During this time, she learned how to support herself and be alone. She neither abandoned her goal, nor did she settle for just any relationship, even if it meant giving up a wealthy man. After one last relationship, she knew she had "passed" her self-imposed "test" and was ready for a healthy relationship.

> I met him at a class reunion and we immediately connected. After listening to me for ten minutes, he said, "You said more from the heart than I have heard from this entire group in the last three hours." The second night I sat at a full table when he entered. Another person asked him to sit with us and he squeezed next to me.

> We both believe this relationship is divinely guided. This is the first class reunion we have attended in thirty years. We both were divorced, came alone, and ended up sitting together. That night I knew this was it.

The fairy tale continued. They grew up two blocks from each other, went to the same high school, and yet never met each other until thirty years later. She planned to go into a convent but didn't. He went to a seminary and left. Their backgrounds were French-Irish. They both loved many of the same things, including Irish music. On their first date, they sang Irish and Broadway music together. A caring, giving, spiritual person, he was her ideal manifestation. They were married less than six months later and now live happily out west.

She does not regret the years that led up to this, even with all the hardships and disappointments. She realizes the relationship came when it did because she was ready for it. "Had it come earlier, I wouldn't have known whom I was and what I wanted to do," she says.

Evidently, an invisible force guides and supports us along a path of maximum learning, even though we often don't recognize it. Sometimes it is dramatic, demanding, and almost harsh, but the intent is always to promote growth and learning. The partners we attract reflect parts of ourselves in need of healing. This woman wanted a very special relationship, but to attract it she first had to be that person herself. As she knows so well, she would not otherwise have been ready and perhaps would not have recognized those qualities she so appreciated.

Choosing Our Experiences

Group members increasingly saw how they attracted each experience by their own thoughts, most of which were unconscious. They examined experiences for clues into their thoughts. Unconscious thoughts are habits that serve useful purposes. How many of us drive home from work and let our minds wander? Perhaps we review all the things that need to be done when suddenly we arrive home. We operated on automatic pilot because we have no recollection of traffic conditions or the mechanics of driving.

We often revert to automatic pilot with other experiences. Choices and reactions are not only habitual but are out of our awareness. Automatic pilot frees up our consciousness to do certain things, since we can't always be weighing and evaluating every decision, but it also limits possibilities.

We may never consider an alternate route or evaluate a troublesome relationship as preparation for a satisfying one. One participant played detective when he felt depressed on cold, rainy days. He noticed that he would think, "What a depressing day." Through manifesting, he knew that his thoughts and moods were connected. He had long associated a rainy day with sadness and boredom. Many past experiences contributed to this. He decided to experiment with his thoughts to change his outlook.

> Now on a rainy and cold day, I say to myself, "What a great time to do all those things that I didn't want to do on a nice day! I feel great and have lots of good energy." I found this hard at first because it wasn't how I felt, but I did it anyway.

> The next week had lots of rainy days. Instead of climbing the walls, I was feeling great and even joyous! I hardly noticed the bad weather. Much to my surprise, it didn't seem to matter. It's so clear to me now: The weather didn't depress me; my choosing to see it that way did.

This person is now paying close attention to his thought pattern. He not only notices what's happening, but what the voice in his head is saying. He later writes:

> It then occurred to me, why wait to detect a message that I didn't like before replacing it? So I just started saying to myself any message I wanted to hear, like: "I have great energy; I am joyous; I am loving; I am prosperous; life flows perfectly; and anything else that felt right." I also found myself being more thankful for all that I have.

> Within three weeks, the change was dramatic. At times I am uncomfortable with so much joy and excitement because I'm not used to it.

We choose how to react. It can be either positive or negative. Whichever we select, we attract more of the same.

Love and Fear

We are constantly presented with opportunities to choose love over fear, to see ways to grow or retreat into fear. One challenge involves learning how to love those who don't love or appreciate us. Loving without expectation of anything in return is called unconditional love. To love on this level is a challenge not only for those involved in manifesting but perhaps for all of humanity.

We close with several illustrations of the transformative nature of love, the most powerful force for change we know. The first involves an elementary school teacher. This woman had a particularly disruptive class, which she said, "tried her patience." She finally adjusted her own attitude instead of blaming them.

> The kids would never settle down and I kept trying different ways to get their attention. I was apprehensive when they arrived. I would think, "Oh, no, here they come." I soon realized that the only reason they were disruptive was because they didn't have any love in their lives. I felt myself opening up and flooding the room with love. I said an affirmation: "These are great kids." I looked at them with unconditional love. I did this for a period of a month. Lo and behold, they settled down, and now they work quietly and seem happy.

In the second and third examples, we have manifestors who could certainly have justified an unloving attitude toward the person causing so much trouble. Instead, they turned their situations into rewarding learning experiences about the transformative power of love.

My first husband, a lawyer, left me when I was pregnant with my fifth child. I had no money, no address, and no job. I returned soda cans for money to feed my kids. I never did get support. He had two kids by his paramour and then ran off with his secretary. He never contacted us for years.

I had a hard life; did anything I could to make money; and sent all my kids through college. The youngest is in the Peace Corps. I'm proud of what I did. Three of my kids reached out to my ex-husband but got a minimal response. I recently learned that his wife left him and he is a ruined man. I felt bad for him. Deep down, he is a very good person.

Over the last six months, I sent him love and light. He joined an alcohol-support program and contacted one daughter whose husband is addicted to pot. He sent her money and a book about codependence. He never did anything like this before. He met with three of my kids and seems to be making some sense of his 59 years.

I worked in a small department with six people. I had a good background for the work and the manager "shined" on me.

A new employee wanted to move up fast by making everyone else look bad. I was his prime target and he was a good street fighter. He attacked me in a roundabout fashion and I even thought it was my imagination at first. I saw only painful options and felt angry.

I couldn't play his game and didn't want to put more energy into dissension or maintaining the same situation.

The message came into my head to love my enemy. How would I do this? I'm not going to give him a big kiss and hug him. I decided to focus on things I could love about him rather than things I was angry about. He did have a good side.

At first it was hard and it was just teeny little things. The more I focused on the good things, the bigger they were in proportion to the others. The tiny good stuff began to out-balance the negative side.

As soon as I got to the point of loving him, all his other games stopped cold. I was glad to see him when I bumped into him. He became my friend, although I didn't want this. It was a very powerful experience. I didn't spend any more time with him than before, but the negativity and dissension disappeared.

Each participant could have easily felt justified in reacting with anger. The schoolteacher could have blamed the parents for their unruly children. She also could have resorted to much stricter discipline.

The divorced mother of five had every reason to resent her former husband, who left her penniless. She felt compassion instead, sent him loving energy, and helped the children get to know him. We have no way of knowing whether her energy directly affected her former husband, but the outcome is promising. She has little doubt of the effect of her prayerful message.

Finally, we have a wonderful example of a situation most of us have found ourselves in at some point. The unhappy coworker could have retaliated. Instead he chose a loving response for his manipulative colleague. We can apply his method to our own situations.

Almost everyone has qualities we appreciate or dislike. We select which characteristics to emphasize and respond to. The more we appreciate someone, the more we find to value. If we choose to see fear, we find that also.

The final two examples illustrate again how we can deal with unpleasant work situations. The transformations are particularly noteworthy with both the recipients and senders of the loving energy.

> My boss had a way of making us all feel uncomfortable. I asked if I could have time off for Christmas. Instead of saying "no" she said, "I don't know where you ever got the idea you could get time off." She acted as if I had done something wrong. She treated everyone this way.
>
> I knew she had a troubled and painful childhood, so I started seeing her with loving light and arms outstretched. I saw her smiling and crying. The hardest time I had was hugging her. I surrounded her with loving energy from my higher self so I didn't actually see my arms doing it.
>
> I saw her with her defenses down. I felt she must be incredibly unhappy. After I quit my job I continued to love her and it was actually easier then. I think she mirrored my own fear and lack of confidence. I healed something because I feel more confident and can actually see myself working for her now.
>
> When I went to the store last week, I noticed what a good mood she was in. My friend said she was really upbeat lately and that everyone commented on this. By the way, only my friend knew of my experiment.

Our office secretary was totally unsuited to her job. She was neither clean nor bright and her clothes were held together with safety pins. A nasal drip made her snort when she talked. Everyone knew she was a disaster except she herself.

In desperation I brought her into my meditative state. I stood in front of her and said, "I love you" and put my arms around her. After doing this I noticed she got smaller and I saw myself at an age when I felt bad about myself. I understood that I had to love that person.

I soon saw that the negative energy around her was gone. I never said anything to this girl but the filing mistakes stopped and she washed her hair regularly. She made an appointment with an allergist and three months later married and left the company. I never told anyone. I did this to rid myself of negativity.

In both cases the senders of love report that they too benefited from the manifestation. They recognized that the annoying person might unwittingly be their teachers and healers. Perhaps the unpleasant colleague catalyzed issues of confidence or anger. At the very least, they could work in a more harmonious environment.

We have choices when faced with unpleasant coworkers. Do we see superficial aspects and then project all kinds of negative characteristics onto that person? For example, if a given person is a Communist, he must be some kind of dangerous aggressor who wants to annihilate us. How quickly that has changed! Were the Russians really all that different before Glasnost?

If we all learn from these examples, we could go a long way toward creating an earth of love, peace, and harmony.

But why not begin within our own orbit and—most impor-
tantly—with ourselves?

Certainly love is the most powerful manifestation of all.

Chapter 9

What We Have Learned

During the early stages of our research, we thought we had discovered a fascinating tool enabling people to create more of what they wanted. In turn, they would enjoy an enhanced quality of life and a higher level of happiness. Instead, a far richer and more complex picture of the consciousness-matter connection surfaced.

Two basic questions emerged: First, how to discover what the relationship really was between thought and matter. Second, how conscious we wished to be of this process, an even more fascinating query. Though the process may be largely subconscious, we actually manifest beliefs and desires all the time. On the one hand, we can remain unaware of the relationship between belief and experience and perhaps perceive ourselves as victims of external circumstances. On the other hand, we can become more conscious of the various ways we create reality. The choice is always ours.

In becoming more conscious, we can also choose among many creative methods. No single approach or rule fits everyone, so we must experiment.

Manifestation techniques have far greater significance than simply materializing thought. The real value is a process that leads to new dimensions of self-discovery and understanding. Simply deciding what to manifest offers insight into what we value. The manifestor who thought the perfect job was one that did not inconvenience her family and paid well was disappointed when she actually got such a position. Only when she acknowledged her own worth and accepted her desire for a meaningful job did she attract more satisfying offers. Not surprisingly—given the many examples we have recorded and participated in ourselves—we now believe we can and do create our experiences.

Nevertheless, we sometimes find ourselves retaining beliefs that simultaneously contradict this principle. Our package of beliefs is neither homogeneous nor consistent, even when we consider only the conscious ones. We've seen so many contradictions that validate the process and confirm our humanity. For example, we can heal a sore elbow or fix a faulty rototiller through conscious desire alone and maintain doubts about this ability.

It may be easy to manifest some things, but not others. The woman who fixed her car without mechanical intervention has been frustrated for years by her inability to attract a lasting romance.

Few of us exposed to these principles don't bring a lifetime of beliefs emphasizing restrictions. Some individuals make major instantaneous changes, but most find an internal structure of limitation.

Our culture typically looks for personal solutions through authorities, particularly governmental and medical institutions. We've been socialized to seek outside answers, so we develop belief systems that are remarkably resistant to change. At times we may find it easier to see ourselves as victims of circumstances, even if this makes us dependent on an external authority. Such a belief becomes self-fulfilling. The more we resist that we create our own reality, the less likely we can.

The status quo can be comforting and reassuring, even when circumstances are miserable. An old adage says, "Better the devil we know than the devil we don't." We mistrust the unknown and fear risking what we already have, however meager it might be. Moreover, our cultural heritage discourages trusting intuitive guidance. Unless we can be objective and rationally certain that some act will translate into a favorable experience, we hesitate to take the risk.

Most of us also have a strong need for validation from others. Acting on the belief that we are the creators of our reality is likely to make us unpopular in a culture that socializes us to dependency and disempowers our capacity to meet our personal needs. This is particularly true if the circumstances for which we assume responsibility are unpleasant, such as an accident, illness, or personal loss. Believing that we need external sources for healing and validation keeps us powerless. Yet this conviction may be intractable, however much we wish to go beyond it. Beliefs provide structure, order, and direction in our daily activities. At the same time, beliefs filter what we see. First, they tell us when to be alert. Second, once we pay attention, they determine our reaction. For example, consider these conflicting perceptions from two retirement-home residents:

A beautiful outdoor swimming pool was situated within the property's bird sanctuary. One resident swam back and forth under the watchful eye of a tall, white bird, waiting to take a drink from the pool. The swimmer stopped and remarked how beautiful and graceful the bird was. Alongside the pool was another resident in a wheelchair who seemed very agitated. Containing herself no longer, she told the swimmer to chase the bird away because it might soil the water. As if sensing its unwelcome, the bird quickly gulped a few mouthfuls of water and flew off.

Here were two women observing the same event. One marveled at a beautiful visitor's presence. The other saw a dirty invader that might soil something she herself was in no condition to use. Each resident conveyed her respective belief system about love and beauty by assessing the same situation with very different "eyes."

We always have a choice: We can become aware of our beliefs or continue to pretend they are inconsequential. In either case, they control the circumstances we attract. By knowing what they are and how they operate, we gain the power to replace those beliefs and circumstances we dislike. We can view life as full of fear and threat or we can choose to perceive it as filled with love, abundance, and beauty. Is it a beautiful bird or an intrusive creature? The choice is ours; what we **see** is what we actually find. Previously, one man looked for things he liked in a colleague and found it easier to notice even more characteristics to like.

If you are unsure about this, simply look at your life and ask what beliefs contribute to your circumstances. Life is a wonderful mirror of our consciousness.

We can view even a negative circumstance as an opportunity for something new and more desirable to take its place. Remember the man who always manifested bad weather on vacation? Later, his awareness paved the way to change. Do you also remember the person who was unable to attend a sold-out concert? He chose not to blame himself or fate for his apparent misfortune. His acceptance then led him to discover another concert and to experience even greater pleasure.

You Do Not Have to Deny Present Beliefs to Embrace New Ones

Change can come in many ways and at different speeds. Some people make dramatic changes following a major crisis, such as a life-threatening illness or a financial disaster. For the rest of us, baby steps accomplish the same results, though perhaps less dramatically.

An important first step is to accept yourself with doubts and counterproductive thinking, as you presently exist. This recognition allows for change. Beliefs built up over a lifetime may have served you well, so you don't have to invalidate them. Changing your thinking can feel threatening, particularly if you try to make them all at once. In fact, don't deny the beliefs you've fortified over the years. Renouncing them illustrates attachment and gives them even more power.

All beliefs limit you to some extent, but some have less potency than others. Moreover, working simultaneously with beliefs that apparently contradict each other can work out. No ideal set of beliefs exists. In the end, what works for you is what counts.

When you accept yourself and your beliefs, you create a gateway for change. Then you can use a variety of techniques and personal experiments, preferably with a dose of humor and detachment. Manifesting works best when it is fun and little ego is invested in the outcome.

A second baby step involves starting small and working from negligible goals to larger ones. If you attempt a big jump—such as healing a serious medical condition through conscious will—you may not really believe you can do it and set yourself up for failure.

Use old standard methods along with new ones. The person with tennis elbow did not immediately cast aside traditional treatment. He gradually weaned himself away from them. Nor did he feel he had personally failed if occasional doubts made him return to regular remedies.

We want to emphasize that beliefs about limitation are not necessarily flawed. Even if you choose to render your present beliefs obsolete, you should recognize and respect them. After all, they got you to this point. Most of all, do not judge yourself. You can retain a belief in lack and simultaneously allow prosperity thinking to surface. If you think that a belief in scarcity is wrong, you end up judging yourself. Just accept it while you simultaneously plant seeds of abundance.

Learning to Enjoy the Process

Like the participants, you can learn to be the architect of your own life. We found joy and became less attached to or consumed by goal fulfillment. In a sense, our objective was to learn about the inner mechanics of the process.

Of course, we cheered when one of us actually did manifest something. Then again, it was equally exciting to recognize ourselves as being part of the flow, when we always arrived at the right place at the desired time. We even marveled when we were hopelessly out of synch, like when the harried driver with no time to spare "happened" to hit every red light and delay imaginable. Goals provide direction, but when we make them the ends in themselves; struggle to achieve; and become attached, we miss most of the pleasure. Worse still, we likely see our goals receding into the distance.

So learn to enjoy the process, which can become wonderfully liberating. View it all as a learning experience. Our group increasingly trusted that all experiences were leading us toward our chosen goals. We even looked upon our setbacks as mysterious steps toward their realization. Indeed, we may retroactively understand their value later. For instance, how could the concert-goer know that being turned away from one concert prepared him for an even more enjoyable experience at another? How could someone—who was unable to find beachside parking—know that 30 minutes later it would rain?

Remember that money, desired experiences, or relationships are byproducts of the process. Attaining them only leads to new goals. A person who always focuses on the end result lives in the future, while missing the joy of the present.

You can also recognize the value of creating a supportive environment in your life in general. You may not belong to a manifestation group but you can become more aware of negative and positive situations and the outlooks of the individuals populating your life. People in the group found themselves reading fewer negative news stories and spending less time with fearful people. We knew that negativity would adversely influence both our thinking and manifestations.

As we learned more, we occasionally speculated on what the world would be like if everyone on the planet believed in abundance and their own self-healing powers? What would this mean for the overburdened and poorly functioning welfare and medical systems? If we all felt we could create what we needed, how might this reduce the level of blame and conflict in families, cities, and national governments? The possibilities for creating layers of prosperity, peace, and well-being were tremendously exciting.

Conclusion

As we conclude this book, we return once more to the question raised earlier: Are any limits imposed on what we can manifest? One part of us believes that no restrictions impede us. Another part is skeptical: Will we ever escape the boundaries of pre-existing and deeply internalized beliefs?

At this point we have no answer. We are even still affected by our deeply entrenched and reinforced concepts. However, this project has gradually "loosened" all of us up. Our thoughts—and the beliefs that instill meaning and value—are a little more visible now than when we began.. We are now more cognizant and freely direct our experiences and interpret events. The whole process was both liberating and educational.

The question will always remain whether there are limitations to what we can create, for there will always be new challenges for us. That is part of what makes this process so intriguing. The attainment of some ultimate goal of manifestation is not what creates our joy and excitement. Rather, it is the ongoing process of working through our limitations and continually surprising ourselves with our own powers of creativity that creates much happiness, fulfillment, and peace.

Afterword

Understanding how the process of manifestation operates in our daily lives is an ongoing exploration. In the sequel to this book, *Manifesting Your Heart's Desire Book II,* the authors ask the question "Assuming we are constantly creating our lives, then what is the significance and larger meaning of some of the major life milestones most of us experience at one time or another?" Once again, the authors draw upon the experiences of participants in the manifestation group as they seek out the value and significance from the challenges they meet in their relationships, jobs or serious illnesses. Were they responsible for these events in their lives as well? And, ultimately, were they manifesting a life they were destined to live?

If you are interested in learning more about manifesting, you can find the authors on the World Wide Web at:

http://www.uvm.edu/~afengler/

This site serves as a way to provide information and stories about manifesting to interested readers as well as permitting questions and comments to be addressed directly to the authors. Visiting the site can facilitate networking with like minded people and also provide information about additional materials related to the subject of manifestation.